THE BEST
CANADIAN POETRY
IN ENGLISH
2018

THE Best Canadian Poetry IN ENGLISH

2018

HOA NGUYEN
GUEST EDITOR

ANITA LAHEY
SERIES EDITOR

BIBLIOASIS
WINDSOR, ONTARIO

FIRST EDITION
Second printing, August 2019

ISBN 978-1-98804-044-8 (Trade Paper)

SERIES EDITOR: Anita Lahey
GUEST EDITOR: Hoa Nguyen
ADVISORY EDITOR: Amanda Jernigan

CONSULTING EDITOR: Molly Peacock
MANAGING EDITOR: Heather Wood
COPY EDITOR: Doyali Islam
COVER AND TEXT DESIGN: David Jang
COVER PHOTO: Keith Bremner

Canada Council for the Arts · Conseil des Arts du Canada

ONTARIO ARTS COUNCIL
CONSEIL DES ARTS DE L'ONTARIO
an Ontario government agency
un organisme du gouvernement de l'Ontario

Canada

ONTARIO CREATES | ONTARIO CRÉATIF

Published with the generous assistance of the Canada Council for the Arts, which last year invested $153 million to bring the arts to Canadians throughout the country, and the financial support of the Government of Canada. Biblioasis also acknowledges the support of the Ontario Arts Council (OAC), an agency of the Government of Ontario, which last year funded 1,709 individual artists and 1,078 organizations in 204 communities across Ontario, for a total of $52.1 million, and the contribution of the Government of Ontario through the Ontario Book Publishing Tax Credit and Ontario Creates.

PRINTED AND BOUND IN CANADA

CONTENTS

POEMS

ANITA LAHEY

Foreword

> *"...the only genuine joy you can have is in those rare moments when you feel that although we may know in part...we are also a part of what we know."*
> *—Northrop Frye, from "The Motive for Metaphor"*

Molly Peacock was ever-so-slightly flustered.

We were at a fête held in Peacock's honour, in appreciation for her decade as series editor of *The Best Canadian Poetry in English*, and for her role as BCP's founding editor. One of her admirers, in a speech of thanks, praised the "institution" Peacock had built.

Peacock stood up. "Well!" she declared, with a flourish and a laugh. Then she confessed she'd always been suspicious of institutions—all institutions, from the family on outward. How surprising, then, to discover she'd gone and created one. I sensed (was I right?) a flicker of dismay: had she done the very thing she most wished, in life, to avoid? I called out, "That is the most rebellious response, Molly!"

"Rebellious" wasn't quite it. What I meant to convey was this: to create a counterweight in an off-balance world is a bold act, one that can foster welcome and lasting change. The new "institution" butts up against older ones, altering their context and their reach. In *The Educated Imagination*, Northrop Frye proposes that our emotional response, as humans, to the world we inhabit, "varies from 'I like this' to 'I don't like this'... Art begins as soon as 'I don't like this' turns into 'this is not the way I could imagine it.'" The anthology you're holding—likewise every poem within it—results from the firing of that nerve, from the impulse of critical consciousness shooting across the synapse, to flex the imaginative muscle.

BCP was conceived in a daring conversation between Peacock and Tightrope's founding publisher, Halli Villegas, about the need for an annual reckoning of and with Canadian poetry. It was brought forth by a nascent, determined small press, then carried onward and built into something tangible and recognized—and *needed*, and now eagerly watched for each year—through sustained vision and pure hard work. That BCP has grown into an entity enduring enough to be termed, even in passing, an "institution," suggests that it rose up to fill a waiting space in our literary landscape.

Molly Peacock shepherded BCP through its first decade by dint of her wisdom, her flare, and her deeply rooted passion for the matter of poetry: its working parts, its adornments, its meanings, and the "matter" of just how *much* it matters. Having brought the anthology this far, Peacock is stepping back. To come forward as successor is, for me, necessarily more than an honour and a privilege. Luckily I've worked closely with her on the anthology for the past four years, time enough to absorb the ethos and adventurous spirit she brought to this annual leap into our poetic wilds.

I won't be alone. I work closely with BCP's marvel behind-the-curtains, managing editor Heather Wood, and I draw on the breadth of literary experience and abiding love for poetics brought by our new advisory editor, Amanda Jernigan. Also, I keenly anticipate working with BCP's new crew of editors-at-large, a rotating team of eyes on the Canadian poetry scene whose input will inform our considerations. Our hope is that those who volunteer to serve as editors-at-large will help us to broaden the anthology's perspective and deepen its reach into sometimes-overlooked pockets of Canlit.

BCP *is* an adventure each year, with each edition's particular guest editor boldly setting the course. But it has moved beyond the experimental phase. It has notched itself into place and has held fast long enough that it now bears some responsibility for the position it's claimed: the manner in which it holds that position and looks out from it, and to some extent the manner in which it's seen.

It's my duty, in the coming years, with the help of readers, contributors and fellow editors, to take stock of this anthology as it, in turn, takes stock of our poetics. As series editor, I aim to step back from it and try to see its true shape. (Please, talk to me. As members of our BCP family, tell me your ideas, your concerns, your thoughts.) I must peer along the walls for cracks that need filling, and for other cracks that deserve to be widened, so fresh light may pour in.

The backbone of this anthology is its annual guest editor: that's who scours the literary landscape for the works that make their way into this book. It's the richness of our guest editors' minds, and the depth of their poetic knowledge, that I most look forward to engaging with each year.

Peacock, too, will be with us, and not just in terms of her legacy. As consulting editor, Peacock remains deeply connected to, and committed to, BCP. Her exuberance shall continue to buoy us, her vision to help steer us, and her depth of experience to steady us.

I'm grateful to have been entrusted with this endeavour, a project that I found thrilling and essential long before my own involvement in its making. And I'm grateful as ever to the poets, and to all who toil at the magazines that publish them.

CB

One of the most tattered anthologies on my shelf is *The Rattle Bag*, edited by Seamus Heaney and Ted Hughes. The cover is a bluish green, and the broad spine of my copy is cracked every few millimetres or so. The joy of this book, aside from its editors' ebullient delight in the powers and charms of language, is its organizing principle. The poems are not arranged thematically or chronologically. Nor are they alphabetized by their authors' names. Instead, the poems follow one upon the other alphabetically by title. This method produces marvellous moments of serendipity. It allows readers to leap whole centuries, and sets them free of any thematic scheme the editors might have been tempted to weave. It subtly bestows primacy on the poem, instead of on its author.

The poems in BCP have always been arranged alphabetically by their authors' last names. This allows for easy skimming if a reader is looking for a piece by a particular poet. As an avid reader of contemporary Canadian poets, I'm sympathetic to this impulse. But when we—the series editors and guest editors—discuss the work at hand, we don't have poets in the room with us. It is us and the poems. We're talking theme, form, metaphor, voice, language, line. So this year we asked ourselves, what if we foregrounded the names of poems instead of the names of poets?

Don't worry, this isn't severe tough love. We aren't making it impossible for you to quickly seek out your favourite poets: we've included an alphabetical index of authors at the back of the book.

It's exciting when we read a poem that feels original, when we encounter an unexpectedly sharp twist that squeezes something as-yet unseen from language or form. Those of us in the editing chair hope to jam-pack an anthology like this with such finds. In her essay collection *Nine Gates: Entering the Mind of Poetry*, American poet Jane Hirshfield reframes originality by suggesting it is, in part, a question: "a request we make of ourselves and the world. We ask it in the quality of our attention and concentration, and we ask it without expectation of an answer."

Once those moments of originality exist, though, they do answer. The nature of their answers will depend upon what needs, what perspectives, what likes and dislikes, and, as Hirshfield puts it, what quality of "concentration and attention" the reader brings to the encounter. These moments of originality also answer one another.

I don't expect readers to get this obsessively involved, but it's interesting to ponder the pairings and successions that result from our new organizing principle. They're tough to parse—the hypothetical associative pathways veer and tangle—but there's no mistaking it: this simple, seemingly minor adjustment makes for a different book. Our tour through the year in Canadian poetry begins with its focus not on a name near the beginning of the alphabet, not on a personality in contemporary Canadian poetry, not on a "new" or familiar voice, but on a word—in this case, "African," the first word in the title of Michael Fraser's poem, "African Canadian in Union Blue."

☙

We are truly fortunate to have guest editor Hoa Nguyen's take on the past year in Canadian poetry. She comes to the task with enthusiasm, openness, and a critical reading eye. As anyone who has studied with Nguyen in her long-running, intensive poetry courses knows, her poetic knowledge and analytical powers run deep, while her love of language and its possibilities—for reshaping meaning; for reconstituting histories and perspectives; and perhaps above all that, for play—is profound.

I leave you now to Nguyen, and to Jernigan—to their respective takes on the echoes that ricochet between the poems here. Their insights don't define this gathering: I heartily encourage you to delve in on your own terms. But their essays do provide richly compelling pathways in. And, just as the poems begin to talk to one another in their proximity, so, too, do these wonderful essays interact—with each other, and with the works that follow.

I began this foreword with an epigraph from Northrop Frye's essay "The

Motive for Metaphor": "...*the only genuine joy you can have is in those rare moments when you feel that although we may know in part...we are also a part of what we know.*" I wish each reader of this year's BCP many such helpings of joy: experiences of the strange and thrilling minglings that happen when you both know "in part," and know that you are a part. In its way, each poem in this collection reminds us of and offers this possibility.

Anita Lahey
Victoria, BC

HOA NGUYEN

The Self-edge of Poetry

My mother used the cotton material to make curtains, I think. I remember the design: stuffed toy bears with large blank eyes next to flat primary-coloured daisies. What interested me then and now is not the curtains she made, not the design or pattern of the material, but the selvage.

Selvage is the far edge of fabric, a made thing of a made thing. It is densely woven, often folded over itself, produced to prevent the fabric from unravelling. It's not meant to be seen—it's meant to be part of the making and, typically, kept out of sight. But the selvage is necessary; it's the background woof, doubled to preserve a pattern. The word selvage, etymologically: self + edge.

I've come to approach poetry as a selvage: a made thing (poems) of a made thing (language). Poems announce their made-ness and reveal themselves as they keep the threads of their making together. They are structural cohesions encoding experience, perception, reflection, knowledge, facts, and events. Like selvage, poems are not made to be "used"—and yet they are essential.

The selvage of that 1970s teddy-bear fabric appeared as a white, thickened band, flat and printed at intervals with lot numbers, revealing the making and maker. Perhaps a poem is a moment of elaboration that requires a kind of doubling, one that exposes and reveals, a band of being and not-being. Existence + a gathered edge.

The band of poems I've assembled here for *The Best Canadian Poetry in English 2018* contains no unified mythology, no conclusive statement on what it means to be best or to be Canadian. If I were to gather the threads into a cohesive self-edge, I would say the themes in this collection bring together threshold attentions: land, globe, language and embedded histories of language; orality and speech; land occupation (the land that is occupied and occupies); sky, water, species; social orders and disorders; love; and spatial and temporal narratives that are spun and spin. They pitch toward rhythm and structure in studied improvisation and manipulation as they assemble contrary histories into words, words that attempt vision and utterance, acknowledgment and registration.

My hope is that these poems gather polyphonic threads of potency, challenge, play, understanding and awareness. My hope is that, like the poems here, poetry gives shape to what can be imagined and reimagined, engaging us as it occasions a shift in perspective.

Thank you to the editors and poets of 2017, when the works here first appeared in print or online, for allowing me to collect this selvage of poems. It has been an honor and pleasure.

Hoa Nguyen
Toronto, ON

AMANDA JERNIGAN

The Crooked Bridge

In Anita Lahey's preface to this year's edition of *The Best Canadian Poetry in English*, she talks about her tattered copy of *The Rattle Bag*, Seamus Heaney's and Ted Hughes's wonderful, deep- and wide-going anthology of poetry in English. I have that on my shelf, too. Picking it up again, today, inspired by Lahey, I think about how, when I read an anthology like this—a poet's (or, in this case, poets') selection of poems—I'm always in some sense reading two ways. I'm looking to see what Hughes and Heaney have to tell me about English-language poetry—but I'm also looking to see what this particular selection of English-language poetry has to tell me about Heaney and Hughes. This kind of double vision enlivens my experience of a book. It has been part of the attraction of BCP for me, down the years: these books, too, are poets' selections of poems.

It's for this reason that I want to bring the poetic voice of guest editor Hoa Nguyen into the anthology (a new gesture, this, for BCP, but one I'd like to make a tradition): to set up at the outset a poem of hers, as a kind of inauguration—not at all to define or confine the selection that follows, but to remind us of the double vision that an anthology like this may draw out of us, adding a stereoscopic dimension to our reading.

DIỆP BEFORE COMPLETION

Her first name
deemed too delicate
for a failing baby

She was a baby failing
(arrived blue   feet first)

Newly named Diệp after the strapping
Chinese butcher

Renamed   she recovers!

She says later
"It's an ugly sounding name"
and thus not popular

I say it wrongly
can't really say it
fake my way

Do we believe in
The Compassionate Protector
of Children?

(The past tense of sing is not singed)

I discovered this poem—just one, of course, in Nguyen's vast, unfolding oeuvre—in the midst of this year's BCP selection process. I found it reprinted as part of an article by Paul Christiansen in the *Saigoneer* about Nguyen's recent work. Reading the article, I was moved to remember how all the work undertaken by guest editors of BCP—the reading, the scanning and photocopying, the weighing and considering, the making of lists, the rereading, the re-listening—happens in the midst of poets' lives, full lives already thronged with commitments: writing, teaching, editing, family, travel. But I was also moved by this poem, in particular, by its song and its fire.

The *Saigoneer* article makes it clear that "Diệp Before Completion" is linked to one of Nguyen's current projects, a project involving the life of her mother—but the mother-daughter connection in the poem itself is drawn with a light touch. A reader encountering this poem in isolation, without the context offered in the *Saigoneer*—for example in its original published form, as a Cuneiform Press broadsheet—might only after multiple readings intuit that the poem is, or could be, in a daughter's voice: "Do we believe in / The Compassionate Protector / of Children?"

The poem's concerns—naming and renaming, protection and belief, the double meanings in language, the present and the past—*are* caught up in the theme of matrilinearity. But they are also multivalent: re-combinative—to use a word that Nguyen deployed in the course of our discussions about her BCP selection—that is, having the faculty of recombination, the ability to put things together in new ways. "The re-combinative possibilities of poetry," she said: as an editor, she is drawn to poems that explore these possibilities. As a poet, she enacts these possibilities, again and again.

Nguyen begins her own preface to this volume with a story of her mother, her mother's making: the selvage of the fabric Nguyen's mother used to make curtains becomes a metaphor for poetry. Nguyen had noted, in our BCP discussions, that matrilinearity recurs as a theme in these poems: the circle of women in Sharron Proulx-Turner's "the longhouse"; the ghostly female "forerunners" in Margaret McLeod's "boneknockers"; the prophetic, disillusioned mothers of Nancy Jo Cullen's "TBH"; among others.

My own presence here—I mean, here writing this introduction—evokes matrilinearity: my mother, now retired, was for more than thirty years the editor of the *New Quarterly*, one of the many little magazines that BCP editors review, year on year. I grew up quite literally surrounded by Canadian literature: the stacks and stacks of manuscripts that my mother would carry around with her—I remember her reading, desperately, in the car, as my sister and I staged territorial battles in the back seat—or pile on the free surfaces in our house; the photocopied forms on which she and her fellow editors would write, sometimes "Yes" or "No," but far more frequently, courageously, "Reread." It is no great surprise that I have wound up in what Richard Sanger, another dyed-in-the-wool poet, calls "the family racket." When Lahey asked me if I would come on board as an advisory editor for BCP, it felt like a homecoming. Canadian poetry in English: my mother tongue.

I think about my mother tongue anew, however, as I read Nguyen's poem. Diệp: this renamed name, this butcher's name, this baby's name, this mother's name. "I say it wrongly / can't really say it / fake my way," the speaker says. As mothers and daughters, as writers and readers, we live in language. But we also live between languages—or between *language*. In language's breaks, its gaps.

My mother likes to tell the story of my first word: "Mum," naturally, the syllable metamorphosing out of a howl as I resisted naptime. Delighted, my mother came running back into my room. She claims that ever since then I've understood the power of language. Language as a bridge, say: a straight line between oneself and the object of one's desire. You say "Mum," and your mother comes running. But language doesn't always work that way. You can say "Mum," and someone else comes: maybe a friend, maybe a stranger. Or maybe no one comes at all.

In her poem "'Astronaut Family'," included in this year's anthology, Shazia Hafiz Ramji writes:

> "Growth and development" sounds like
> something my mom used to worry about
> when I was little. Now I say it
> when applying for grants. Before that
> one of my favourite dead people told me
> that it begins with language. Since then
> I have found lots of dead friends

saying the same thing in different ways.
What was once my mom's, then mine,
then mine through the words of others
are now the words of the forthcoming
Lululemon on Hastings Street, Escala
luxury homes in Burnaby....

Now I am a mother myself. I don't always come when my children call me. Sometimes, I am afraid to say, I am too busy reading poems.

❦

"Mum," says my son Anson to me, as we are walking home, "When a seagull says 'friend,' in seagull language, does his friend come?" Yes, I say, seagulls know how to talk to each other. "Do they know how to talk to fish?" he asks.

❦

Language comes to us not just from our mothers but from our fathers, from our friends (the dead and the living), from our lovers, from our writers—from our children—and it is not always given gently. Here is the beginning of Yusuf Saadi's poem "Belittle," also from this year's anthology:

Belittle

I learned that word when you confessed
your dad belittled your puny, puny heart
with fists that smoldered through the night.
And the word *hence*—which you applied
in essays to reach conclusions—now whenever
I write hence, having exhausted *thus, therefore,
consequently*, it reminds me of you. It's strange
how a person claims a word, owns a piece of
language for us. The way Yeats owns *terrible*
for me, as in terrible beauty, or Rumi owns
beloved for you, as in beloved let me enter.
How *lump* is the hospital smell when an aunt
had cancer or *plummet's* full of accident
and the smack of limbs against the waves.
If a word is tainted with story, language
will always be a crooked bridge.

[...]

If a word is tainted with story, language / will always be a crooked bridge. Or, as Bardia Sinaee puts it,

> beware of what
> what you say
> says about you
>
> in this way all poems are true
> even the ugly ones

CB

As Nguyen says, the band of poems assembled here contains no unified mythology, and makes no conclusive statement. But there are recurring themes, and also recurring images. The crooked bridge of language, as in Saadi's poem. The bridge that "arcs like two arms joined / hand-to-wrist or fern-to-lookout," in Robin Richardson's poem "Disembodied At The Botanical Gardens." The "Capitol's bridges" in George Elliott Clarke's "Lincoln Plans for Peace ...," beneath which the water may run apocalyptically red. The bridge in Selina Boan's "inside the vein:," beneath which the tiptoeing moss crosses, surreptitiously. All these bridges, and beneath them, the rivers.

Sometimes the bridges are language; sometimes the rivers are language, too.

Also, sometimes the bridges (and the rivers) are blood: spilled blood, as in Clarke's poem of the civil war, or in Jordan Abel's poem "the tumbling water washes bones"—but also, as in Boan, the blood that runs "inside our veins," the kinship ties that connect us to the mothers and fathers who came before us. In one of the two epigraphs that flank Boan's poem, Bonita Lawrence writes: "For a people who have had much of their knowledge of the past severed, blood memory promises a direct link to the lives of our ancestors." *Is that true?* Boan's poem seems to ask, testing this axiom on the pulse of lived experience. The bridges of blood can be strong as DNA, as in Anne Marie Todkill's poem "November, Stormont County," where the X and Y of migrating geese morph into a unisoned V:

> a chromosome-crossing, X and Y,
> breaking and repairing until the glyph appears,
> aerodynamic letterform for followfollowfollow ...

They can also be as crooked as the bridges of language: "all that fucking," writes Catriona Wright in her poem "Origin Story," the beautiful and the ugly, the consensual and the nonconsensual, "creating and creating and creating and creating / you."

The bridges of blood and language themselves are crisscrossed, bound together in a double helix that is constantly forming, reforming, deforming, informing. I think of the umbilical cord that is both blood and language, in waaseyaa'sin christine sy's poem "my umbilical cord, map trail seasonal camp…," this beautiful "poetics of work." It is a poem of "the precariousness, the fragility of re-relationing kinship ties"; but it is also a poem about the power of heartwork to re-relation; and it is itself a re-relationing:

> this is not a poem.
> this is not an award nomination.
> it is not a contest submission.
>
> this is not a haunting.
> this is neither obituary nor personal legacy.
> it is not a smudge, sweatlodge, or shaking tent.
>
> this is the poetics of one umbilical cord unburying
>   anishinaabe country.
> it's oral history alive + living for the future.

Set your feet upon the crooked bridge. How do you cross it? With exuberance, dancing, as in Daniel David Moses. With "an act of love," as in Ramji. With money (as sy reminds us, "in a capitalist world, relationing costs money"). In flight, as in Chaulk. In song, as in L'Abbé. In a truck (Howard), a train (Quartermain), a wooden horse (Goyette), a space probe (Couture). With a customs declaration (Tubbs). Without a name (Liem). Embodied (Belcourt) or disembodied (Richardson). In a Godzilla suit (Moses, again). In Union Blue (Fraser). With a god (Murakami). With a hookless line (Hall). On foot (Fraser, again), or on hoof (Paré), or with compound eyes, winged (Simmers). With a handful of dust (Islam). At irregular intervals (Warrener). By folding, so that one shore meets the other (Tysdal). This is not an exhaustive list. By becoming the bridge. By becoming the river. You cross the crooked bridge. You cross, and sometimes you fall.

Amanda Jernigan
Hamilton, ON

2018

MICHAEL FRASER ⚬

African Canadian in Union Blue

I was AWOL, an unpaid ridge runner, hawking
distance from the coal-shaded Fifty-fourth
Massachusetts, pulling fleet foot through night
brush, my feet bramble-clawed and day-sore
yowling for a pair of spendy cruisers.
Bounty men near caught me in tamarack
larch. I saw their smoothbore guns day clear,
their eyes haired-up and owly. I was hanging
by my eyelids and angled abeam through
light-blazed meadow balm, jumping log cob
and bull stumps, moss-bitten rot-hole fallers,
deploying all the natural speed my buck-bred
seed-folk gave me. I was baseborn in Chatham,
mammy giving life to six pin-baskets in a rickety
pushcart. If I were to see him now, I'd ask daddy
why he heeled-off before eyeing me wrapped in
scrapped yarn. His master named him John, echoing
the new testament, and what mammy's broken water
branded me. Whitney's cotton gin nearly snapped
his Hamitic saddle-brown back half open. Some days
he bleated raw like a crushed side-born calf, sliding
away from full breath. Heard he upped and skyrooted
through Virginia pine faster than whiskey jacks whistling
over feed camps, and sparked mammy's teenage
mind before stone-rolling to his novel life, a rail toad
booming around rusted aged jimmys and ragshag
toonerville trolleys. I continued dim-moon travelling
west through puckerbush, sledge, and prick-filled
tanglewood, lodging with other lucked-out negroes
beside slick calm finger lakes, hauling soaked rick to
hem-load tipcarts. We'd light down to chew tuff
cow-greased pone before snacking tobacco ropes,
our smoky tea-skinned black bodies day-whipped
and legged out. White clodhopper abolitionists and
schoolmarms let me sleep on shakedowns and boil-up
my battered threads out back, stooped over hose bibbs,
rubboards, or wind-turned mill wash. A swamp Yankee

and his jake leg wife above Rochester stodged up
scrapple, fire-burnt tunkup, and slack salted Pope's nose.
We popped it down with overproof lamp oil and everyone
was all in, plow shined. My mind was so jag skated,
I talked all my closed business like I was up a redwood
tree. Can't extract when my head clunked the sewed-rag
shuck bed. I night-woke bedfast with scarlet runners
beetling my bare flesh. Sweat runnelled and rilled
either side of my chest hillslopes. Heard hushed words
and realised they were studying to forlay me to sellers.
Morning I pretended to smudge along, then lit
out crow-quick past tumps and shadebark glades of
knurled hickory. On the final night, I met bullhorn
thunderheads throwing froth-smurred gulley washers
and stump-mover skies. I squinched and child-stivered
through teeming chizzly freshets that sizzled and gaffed me,
the mud water pooling the path's apron. Almost done in,
I saw America's back forty sproutland, sun-glimming
and drying after the rains had sugared-off. I went down
the ravine scoop smiling towards birlers and their floaty
Niagara chuck boats, waiting to river cross into Canaan.

from *enRoute*

ELI TAREQ LYNCH ∞

After Samiya Bashir's Field Theories

you know like how we sit in a room
together telling stories of diaspora
or sometimes no diaspora at all
been here forever
you know like we are all in
competition, wanna be the model minority, a myth
that ties us together and yet cuts
the link, i am better, no i am better, no I am
closer to being white. you know like how
anti blackness is rampant in most communities
of colour, and you know like how we sometimes
forget that indigenous people exist THEY EXIST
WE ARE ON OCCUPIED LAND or you know like how
we forget who we are
fighting. we need to do better. we always need to do better.

you know like how we sit in a room, drinking chai
tea, laughing, crying, the works, you know like how our best
home is in communities mixed, you know like how
denise's mother in master of none tells young denise and dev
that they are both minorities, you gotta stick together
you know like how many times do you see multiple people of colour
in a show and you know like how many times are they friends?
Lilla Watson says "if you've come because your liberation is
bound up with mine, then let us work together" and we keep
having to quote her, you know like how we have to remind each other
everyday, what is social responsibility, keep each other close,
keep each other safe, you know like how I tell C I want to
write a love poem to all my friends of colour and you know like
how it doesn't ever feel like enough
you know like how i'm sick from
disposability culture, just want to hold you all close
you know like how my communities of colour have healed
me, and not just scratches, but you know like deep wounds
tended to, blood wiped, stitches sewn, large bandages
left to protect, and you know like how we know
the wound will return but we keep trying to heal it

from *The Puritan*

DANIEL DAVID MOSES ☙

The Amerindian in the Godzilla Suit

1.

A prominence divorced from the sun, coming down
To earth like a god or monster in a vision

Everyone's forced to have, but this time, in lieu of
Turning soil into cinders, this tongue of forked

Fire, this dark wing with edges sharp as swords cleaves
Into the polar ice of ages past and calves

Into the once again upon our times bergs and
Brash and a creature part dragon, part anguish.

2.

You think this is the dream Einstein was hoping for,
That he foresaw hydrogen in bed with itself,

Conceiving a light not of this earth? Not the sort
A thought experiment ought to set loose. Hotter

Now than Hiroshima or Nagasaki which
Happened first, which we're still turning over, burning

In our minds, trying out other experiments,
Thoughts, conceptions —which is why we're pulling this old

Tarnished dragon from the ice, stretching skin tall as
A skyscraper, letting it breathe hot as a jet.

And now we find Dene men carried the pitchblende
From Canada and died of radiation too.

Their ghosts glow, restless aurora borealis,
Looking for forgiveness for their part in the crime.

Forgive their ignorance. They haunt Hiroshima,
Nagasaki, the world. One of them wants the job.

3.

How tiny Mount Fuji, how little are earthquakes
Once a great dragon takes the stage. Please allow me.

Forever I've been one of the invisibles.
I'll whip off my blacks and do the dragon's dance.

I promise to honour its magnificence and
Its strange regalia. I know about magic,

Know the very wrist jerk you need to pull those loose
Leather pants on—tada!—both trouser legs at once.

Yes, it's partly clown and part Tyrannosaurus
Rex, a parody of charisma sans the sex.

Give me the chance to make that entrance, to go live
On the screen in that green wrinkling kimono,

To draw breath like a long sword or fire, to fan
The claws out, one who almost loses his balance

And his composure to his own behind, stepping
Onto the city with the gait of a geisha.

My tummy and tail and untouchable skin
Condition might inspire amusement and pity.

But my eyes with pupils vertical slits, my teeth
Long knives, will forfend identification.

Let me step from behind the red curtain, complete
The radioactive invention with rhythmic

Feet. Abbreviated arms will embrace the snakes
Of electric power lines snapping free, sparking

Between towers. Leaping lizard? Let it be me,
Tall as a thunderhead, dancing around the downed

Town of Tokyo. Oh great samurai nation, you
Know these moves, the war dance repurposed for peace.

You're my audience, you who did die and you who
Haven't yet. And you who will be born. Understand.

With your forgiveness, your kind permission, we dead
Will finally exit beyond the black curtain.

from *Arc Poetry Magazine*

TESS LIEM ✣

Anonymous Woman Elegy

The story is about the woman who comes into a cafe
three times a week.

It is about how she is a woman
but is not given a name.

It is about how she died.
About not knowing the woman's name

until she died.
About gathering with strangers to mourn.

It is about the morning the woman died.
The story is about how the woman smiled.

Her teeth.
It is about whether she had a lover,

whether she was loved
whether she deserved love.

Then suddenly the story is about how the narrator feels
bad about the time she told her mother she hated her.

About whether the narrator deserves love.
For a moment, about the woman.

For another, about everyone. But mainly
the story is about the narrator:

how she can make anything
about anyone

about herself seem like
it's about everyone for a moment.

from *carte blanche*

LIZ HOWARD ⳩

As if Our Future Past Bore a Bad Algorithm

A few particles ambushed the past
I opened my mouth to laugh and laughter
Fell from the television
I said to myself
It's almost better than real sugar
This happened yesterday as I traded
My own scalp for grain

Gold loaded our skulls
Onto the backs of the born
And no credit was given
Where no credit was due

Expectation
Having grown so heavy
In its crawl space

*

In between accident and arrival
We are suspended
A significant horizon of downcast gold
In a public moment
My head tilted to the side
Like, what?
The cogito
Is the body
Is nature
Is the backward glancing continuum of Western History
Writ in blood?

It's as if these winters ain't got nothing on a chin
Tilted upward
Speaking plainly it is easier to tide
The lunar part
We are bound
And the world is what I can feel

Up against this boundary
The sentence
Becomes my future mail, my student debt
These heads of nine crows I retreat
Into storage

Scrolling through the temple of your name
I become locked into the commute of this
Falling night
Still dressed for the office
With my thighs awake
As if any art could reify
What time has taken away
The fact so brief I could not see
The temporal bind in front
Of my face

*

History could be
My mother smoking in her truck
Out a cracked window
The bluish greys eddying
Toward escape as the stars
Fly ever farther away
In some other galaxy
Bloodstream cyanide and strange quarks
The half-truth I never know

In another history
My adoptive great-grandmother sleeps on a bed of hay
As the night sky screams a green light of solar rays
In yet another
My birth great-grandmother picks burrs from her worn skirt
In a shack at the edge of the reservation
A moose has been got but where does she go
For her water?
Here I am filming my mother this past summer
Demonstrating for a young cousin how to witch
For a well:
Hold a saw by its edge with both hands

And bring the handle up to your chest
Let it fall then count the bounces
That's how many feet down the water is

*

The future history of mind
Takes everything to forgive
The impulse
Its muted edges grow into a torrent
Of hematic reds and cresyl violet
A dye that finds the stuff of nerves
I cannot make peace with that
Which will not leave me
To test the surface tension of any blue
If I hollow the morrow could you love me
As the poppet of your youth?
I can make an occasion of the hour known as 3AM
For us to seep so readily into confusion
A young man pisses on the sidewalk in front of us
Unknowingly
Pushing a gasp up from his throat before he cuts
And runs down the residential street
Could it be that I've lived too long
With an idle mouth and my boots untied?
The bones of some medieval boy
Discovered in the dying lips
Of an uprooted tree
Call me a taxi when the dawn is incendiary
The green of this has never known me
Not entirely

Dream apartments I was not allowed to rent
The sun hunts me and everything I hold against my sense

from *CV2*

SHAZIA HAFIZ RAMJI ❧

"Astronaut Family"

for my friends who have left Vancouver

"Growth and development" sounds like
something my mom used to worry about
when I was little. Now I say it
when applying for grants. Before that
one of my favourite dead people told me
that it begins with language. Since then
I have found lots of dead friends
saying the same thing in different ways.
What was once my mom's, then mine,
then mine through the words of others
are now the words of the forthcoming
Lululemon on Hastings Street, Escala luxury
homes in Burnaby. This is the quality of dust.
It filters through us, because we're made of it,
the language I mean, my friends know it too
when they land in Los Angeles, Montreal,
New York. No wonder we bought
New Balance before parting ways,
making excuses for the comfort worn by our grandparents—
this is the quality of dust: it takes us dancing
into houses and galleries until six in the morning,
it keeps us here, this expensively repressed sympathy
in sneakers and secret locations that separate us,
like when I message you on Facebook, and it's three in the morning
but seven for you, but you gotta go because you're writing
a condo ad for work, even in Brooklyn and Toronto, even though
it started here where we began to love each other, and I think that we still do
because we come back every summer, and the smiles come increasingly quick—
which is not to say that we're eager to meet, or that this is the sudden light
of friendship, but more than this—this is the construction of an act of love.

from *Canadian Literature*

YUSUF SAADI ☙

Belittle

I learned that word when you confessed
your dad belittled your puny, puny heart
with fists that smouldered through the night.
And the word *hence*—which you applied
in essays to reach conclusions—now whenever
I write *hence*, having exhausted *thus, therefore,*
consequently, it reminds me of you. It's strange
how a person claims a word, owns a piece of
language for us. The way Yeats owns *terrible*
for me, as in terrible beauty, or Rumi owns
beloved for you, as in beloved let me enter.
How *lump* is the hospital smell when an aunt
had cancer or *plummet's* full of accident
and the smack of limbs against the waves.
If a word is tainted with story
language will always be a crooked bridge.

As you fade further in memory, I'll forget
the timbre your voice reached when you wept
and lose the scars above your nose (already
I've forgotten their shapes). Hence, the rare
times I'll think of you will be chance encounters
in novels, poems, or essays which flaunt
those grown-up, guilty words.

from *HA&L magazine*

DIONNE BRAND ❧

from The Blue Clerk

Verso 1 *The back of a leaf*

What is said and what is unsaid; what is written and what is withheld. What is withheld is on the left-hand page. These are left-hand pages. The moment they are written they will not exist. That is, they will not exist as themselves. As they were first conceived. What is withheld is on the back of the leaf.

I have withheld more than I have written. I have restrained more than I have given. I have left unsaid more than I have said. I have withheld much more than I have withheld. Even these nine left-handed pages have already created their own left-handed pages, as will be seen. I will have added for clarification or withdrawn some detail. I will have parsed the structure of the sentence and the meaning of the sentence and reformulated it to resolve some understanding that was tentative in the first place but that merely for the sake of agreeing to a rule of syntax I have to present as certain. Moreover, I will have cleaned out all of my doubt, or all of my prevarication, or all of my timidity.

The left-hand page is a recursive page; each verso becomes a recto. Each left-handed page generates one right-handed page and an infinite number of left-handed pages.

What is withheld multiplies. The left-handed pages accumulate with more speed and intensity than the right-handed pages.

They are chronic. That is to say, they are always present, occurring, intrinsic and incurable, unfailing and uneasy like freight. The freight of withholding, gathered over years, becomes heavier and heavier. Indefinite and unbounded weight.

Verso 1.1

There are bales of paper on a wharf somewhere, at a port, somewhere. There is a clerk inspecting and inspecting them. She is the blue clerk. She is dressed in a blue ink coat, her right hand is dry, her left hand is dripping; she is expecting a ship, she is preparing for one. Though she is afraid that by the time the ship arrives the stowage will have overtaken the wharf.

The sea off the port is roiling some days, calm some days.

Up and down the wharf she examines the bales, shifts old left-handed pages to the back, making room for the swift voluminous incoming freight.

The clerk looks out sometimes over the roiling sea or over the calm sea, finding the horizon, seeking the transfiguration of the ship.

The bales have been piling up for years yet they look brightly scored, crisp and sharp. They have abilities the clerk is forever curtailing and marshalling. They are stacked deep and high and the clerk, in her inky garment, weaves in and out of them checking and rechecking that they do not find their way into the right-hand page. She scrutinises the manifest hourly, the contents and sequence of loading. She keeps account of cubic metres of senses, perceptions and resistant facts. No one need be aware of these, no one is likely to understand, some of these are quite dangerous and some of them are too delicate and beautiful for the present world.

There are green unclassified aphids for example living with these papers.

The sky over the wharf is a sometimish sky, it changes with the moods and anxieties of the clerk, it is ink blue as her coat or grey as the sea or pink as the evening clouds.

The sun is like a red wasp that flies in and out of the clerk's ear. It escapes the clerk's flapping arms.

The clerk would like a cool moon but all the weather depends on the left-handed pages. All the acridity in the salt air, all the waft of almonds and seaweed, all the sharp poisonous odour of time.

The left-handed pages swell like dunes some years. It is all the clerk can do to mount them with her theodolite, to survey their divergent lines of intention. These dunes would envelop her as well as the world if she were not the ink-drenched clerk.

Some years the aridity of the left-hand pages makes the air dusty, parches the hand of the clerk. The dock is then a desert, the bales turned to sand and the clerk must arrange each grain in the correct order, humidify them with her breath and wait for the season to pass.

And some years the pages absorb all the water in the air becoming like four-hundred-year-old wood and the dock weeps and creaks and the clerk's garment sweeps sodden through the bales and the clerk weeps and wonders why she is here and when will the ship ever arrive.

I am the clerk, overwhelmed by the left-handed page. Each blooming quire contains a thought selected out of many reams of thoughts and vetted by the clerk, then presented to the author. The clerk replaces the file, which has grown to a size, unimaginable.

I am the author in charge of the ink-stained clerk pacing the dock. I record the right-hand page. I do nothing really because what I do is clean. I forget the bales of paper fastened to the dock and the weather doesn't bother me. I choose the presentable things, the beautiful things. And I enjoy them sometimes, if not for the clerk.

The clerk has the worry and the damp thoughts, and the arid thoughts.

Now where will I put that new folio. There's no room where it came from, it's withheld so much this time, so much about … this and that …never mind;

that will only make it worse.

The clerk goes balancing the newly withheld pages across the ink-slippery dock. She throws an eye on the still sea; the weather is concrete today, her garment is stiff like marl today.

Verso 1.1.01

When Borges says he remembers his father's library in Buenos Aires, the gaslight, the shelves and the voice of his father reciting Keats' 'Ode to a Nightingale', I recall the library at the roundabout on Harris Promenade. The library near the Metro Cinema and the Woolworths store. But to go back, first when my eyes lit on Borges' dissertation, I thought, 'I had no library.' And I thought it with my usual melancholy and next my usual pride in being without.

And the first image that came to me after that was my grandfather's face with his tortoiseshell spectacles and his weeping left eye and his white shirt and his dark seamed trousers and his newspaper and his moustache and his clips around his shirt arms and his notebooks and his logbooks; and at the same moment that the melancholy came it was quickly brushed aside by the thought that he was my library.

In his notebooks, my grandfather logged hundredweight of copra, pounds of chick feed and manure; the health of horses, the nails for their iron shoes; the acreages of coconut and tania; the nuisance of heliconia; the depth of two rivers; the length of a rainy season.

Then I returned to the Harris Promenade and the white library with wide steps, but when I ask, there was no white library with wide steps, they tell me, but an ochre library at a corner with great steps leading up. What made me think it was a white library? The St Paul's Anglican Church anchoring the lime-white Promenade, the colonial white courthouse, the grey-white public hospital overlooking the sea? I borrowed a book at that white library even though the library as I imagine it now did not exist. A book by Gerald Durrell, namely, *My Family and Other Animals*. I don't remember any other books I brought home, though I remember a feeling of quiet luxury and a desire for spectacles to seem as intelligent as my grandfather. And I read too in this white library a scrap about Don Quixote and Sancho Panza, though only the kind of scrap, the kind of refuse, or onion skin, they give schoolchildren in colonial countries about a strange skinny man on a horse with a round sidekick.

The ochre library on Harris Promenade was at the spot that was called 'library corner' and it used to be very difficult to get to because of the traffic and the narrow sidewalk. But I was agile and small. And I thought I was ascending a wide white-stepped library. And though that was long ago, I remember the square clock adjacent to the roundabout. And I can see the Indian cinema next door, papered with the film *Aarti* starring Meena Kumari and Ashok Kumar.

My grandfather with his logs and notebooks lived in a town by the sea. That sea was like a lucent page to the left of the office where my grandfather kept his logs and notebooks with their accounts. Apart from the depth of the two rivers, namely the Iguana and the Pilot, he also noted the tides and the times of their rising and falling.

ßmoon rise	5.34 a.m.	
high tide	5.48 a.m.	0.82 ft
sunrise	5.56 a.m.	
low tide	12.40 p.m.	0.03 ft
new moon	4.45 p.m.	
sunset	6.23 p.m.	
high tide	6.33 p.m.	0.56 ft
low tide	12.02 a.m.	0.16 ft

Spring tides, the greatest change between high and low, neap tides, the least.

And, the rain, the number of inches and its absence. He needed to know about the rain for sunning and drying the copra. And, too, he kept a log of the sun, where it would be and at what hour, and its angle to the Earth in what season. And come to think of it he must have logged the clouds moving in. He said that the rain always came in from the sea. The clouds moving in were a constant worry. I remember the rain sweeping in, pelting down like stones. That is how it used to be said, the rain is pelting down like stones. He filled many logbooks with rain and its types: showers, sprinkles, deluges, slanted, boulders, sheets, needles, slivers, peppers. Cumulonimbus clouds. Or, nimbostratus clouds. Convection rain and relief rain. Relief rain he wrote in his logbook in his small office, and the rain came in from the sea like pepper, then pebbles, then boulders. It drove into his window and disturbed his logs with its winds and it wet his desk. And he or someone else would say, 'But look at rain!' And someone else would say, 'See what the rain do?' As if the rain were human. Or they would say, 'Don't let that rain come in here.' As if the rain were a creature.

Anyway, my grandfather had a full and thorough record of clouds and their seasons and their violence.

From under the sea a liquid hand would turn a liquid page each eight seconds. This page would make its way to the shore and make its way back. Sometimes pens would wash up onto the beach, long stem-like organic styli. We called them pens; what tree or plant or reef they came from we did not know. But some days the beach at Guaya would be full of these styli just as some nights the beach would be full of blue crabs. Which reminds me now of

García Márquez's old man with wings but didn't then as I did not know García Márquez then and our blue crabs had nothing to do with him; it is only now that the crabs in his story have overwhelmed my memory. It is only now that my blue night crabs have overwhelmed his story. Anyway we would take these pens and sign our names, and the names of those we loved, along the length of the beach. Of course these names rubbed out quickly and as fast as we could write them the surf consumed them. And later I learned those pens were *Rhizophora mangle* propagules.

What does this have to do with Borges? Nothing at all. I walked into the library and it was raining rain and my grandfather's logs were there, and the wooden window was open. As soon as I opened the door, down the white steps came the deluge. If I could not read I would have drowned.

Now you are sounding like me, the clerk says. I am you, the author says.

Verso 4 *To Verse, to Turn, to Bend, to plough, a furrow, a row, to turn around, toward, to traverse.*

When I was nine coming home one day from school, I stood at the top of my street and looked down its gentle incline, toward my house obscured by a small bend, taking in the dipping line of the two-bedroom scheme of houses, called Mon Repos, my rest. But there I've strayed too far from the immediate intention. When I was nine coming home from school one day, I stood at the top of my street and knew, and felt, and sensed looking down the gentle incline with the small houses and their hibiscus fences, their rose-bush fences, their ixora fences, their yellow and pink and blue paint washes; the shoemaker on the left upper street, the dressmaker on the lower left and way to the bottom the park and the deep culvert where a boy on a bike pushed me and one of my aunts took a stick to his mother's door. Again when I was nine coming home one day in my brown overall uniform with the white blouse, I stood on the top of my street knowing, coming to know in that instant when the sun was in its four o'clock phase and looking down I could see open windows and doors and front door curtains flying out. I was nine and I stood at the top of the street for no reason except to make the descent of the gentle incline toward my house where I lived with everyone and everything in the world, my sisters and my cousins were with me, we had our book bags and our four o'clock hunger with us and our grandmother and everything we loved in the world were waiting in the yellow-washed house, there was a hibiscus hedge and a buttercup bush and zinnias waiting and for several moments all this seemed to drift toward the past; again when I was nine and stood at the head of my street and looked down the gentle incline toward my house in the four o'clock coming-home sunlight, it came over me that I was not going to live here all my life, that I was going away and never returning some day. A small wind brushed everything or perhaps it did not but afterward I added a small wind because of that convention in movies, but something like a wave of air, or a wave of time passed over the small street or my eyes, and my heart could not believe my observation, a small wind passed over my heart drying it and I didn't descend the gentle incline and go home to my house and my grandmother and tell her what had happened, I didn't enter the house that was washed with yellow distemper that we had painted on the previous Christmas, I didn't enter the house and tell her how frightened I was by the thought I had at the top of our street, the thought of never living there which seemed as if it meant never having existed, or never having known her, I never told her the melancholy I felt or the intrusion the thought represented. I never descended that gentle incline of the street toward my house, the I who I was before that day went another way, she disappeared and became the I that continued on to become who I am. I do not know what became of her, where she went, the former I, who separated once we came to the top of the street and looked down and something like a breeze that would be added later after watching many movies, passed over us. What became of her, the one who gave in so easily or was she so surprised to find that thought that would overwhelm her so, and what made her keep quiet. When I was nine and coming home one day my street changed just as I stood at the top of it and I knew I would never live there again or all my life. The thought altered the afternoon and my life and after that I was in a hurry to leave. There was another consciousness waiting for a little girl to grow up and think future thoughts, waiting for some years to pass and some obligatory life to be lived until I would arrive here. When I was nine I left myself and entered myself. It was at the top of the street, the street was called McGillvray Street, the number was twenty-one, there were zinnias in the front yard and a buttercup bush with milky sticky pistils we used to stick on our faces. After that all the real voices around me became subdued and I was impatient and dissatisfied with everything, I was hurrying to my life and I stood outside of my life. I never arrived at my life, my life became always standing outside of my life and looking down its incline and seeing the houses as if in a daze. It was a breeze, not a wind, a kind of slowing of the air, not a breeze, a suspension of the air when I was nine standing at the top of McGillvray Street about to say something I don't know what and turning about to run down ... no, my grandmother said never to run pell-mell down the street toward the house as ill-behaved people would, so I was about to say something, to collect my cousins and sisters into an orderly file and to walk down to our hibiscus-fenced house with the yellow outer walls and my whole life inside. A small bit of air took me away.

from *Granta*

MARGARET MCLEOD ✂

boneknockers

I believe in forerunners

my mother's aunt once woke to see her father
at the end of her bed   smiling with sharp teeth
he faded and she knew he was dead at last
the old bastard

Aunt Liz knew when the phone was going to ring
was quick to your doorstep before you even knew you were sick
shivered when a goose stepped over your grave

when I was a girl we heard them   my mother and I
boneknockers   right here one night in late August
we were crossing from the church hall on a Friday evening
just a touch of the cold winds to come   and the crickets crying

then we heard the bones
clicking together
click   click   click
just like that
before and behind and all around us

my mother grabbed my hand so hard I cried
and she dragged me out of this field and down that road over there
me scared of the bone knockers and scareder
that if I fell she wouldn't let go   and my wrist would twist and break
funny what you think about

soon as we got home my mother phoned her aunt
Aunt Liz said there'd be a death before the snow fell

soon everyone was hearing the knocking of bony fingers
all through the rest of August and into September
and Aunt Liz was right

before the next full moon she herself was dead
even now they say she walks that road over there
when the moon is right
her short stubby fingers
grown long in the grave

from *The Antigonish Review*

MIKE CHAULK ❧

The Canada Goose

The Canada Goose can live 23.5 years; grows up
in Southwestern Ontario mostly, a distance of
from; slowly though earlier than most butts up
against its skin; comes home one day from
school and asks its mother why it and Ralph are
the only two black kids in its class, like why is it
black and why is Ralph black and why are they
the only ones, to which its mother responds that
Ralph is Filipino, and that it itself, laughs, is not
black at all—this becoming a family joke; would
tell others its age when asked what it was, where
from, that it just tans real easy, that it can't help it,
and moves its forearm into the shade; denies;
learns later or understands then, as no secret,
that it is a good percent, all this time a good
percent, and its skin a good precent, and half its
family and so on and finally its father put in the
work, the bureaucratic hassle of getting his status
after all them years and time away from
Labrador, his young career flying Otters and
Beavers in and out of camps, in and out of
Rigolet, Nain, Makkovik, Hopedale, you name it
he was flying there and even his own time at
camp, the hunts, trapping, the trip he took with it
to Mulligan, on Lake Melville some hours out of
Goose Bay where ducks were killed, posed with
and rifles, a moose on the river, them all in the
canoe: the father, the grandfather who grew up in
North West River and like a legend to it lived hard
off those he hunted and trapped and caribou
ringalls and bakeapples, like yes b'y, like the kid's
gotta experience all this, as it should and did and
cries when its GameBoy loses charge, like yes
b'y you're too far out if the smell at the stove's
getting to you like that, the game meat, your
GameBoy, the loneliness of the woods at night,
the sting and drag of flies lifting chunks from that

skin, the Big Land——; never talked about it too much until later learned, it being then, it thought, up against its friends and parties and a more or less passable difference; said it just tans real easy; said it never burns, just tans, always tans; says now this fact, the fact of its skin because some percent Inuit, some Cree; says with love now; says without knowing how to say it right, born far from, out of; says it proud though hesitates at times; learns and never learns enough or feels quite; tans, yes; dies.

from *The Malahat Review*

IAN WILLIAMS ❦

Cart

                  were skins By the sixth time
we met we. happened very quickly The progression to nekkid.
held the handle of the oven for balance While removing my socks
I. beheld me as you shed your clothes near the nightlight
in the hallway You. wouldn't call it stripping I. didn't I.
And the evening and the morning were the sixth day.
In that order.

                   during the night
Daylight savings time ended. into end times We fell.
Where were you child when you oughta been prayin'
all on that day? Nina Simone was singing. the bedroom
We couldn't say. ourselves with aprons of fig leaves
We covered. Who told thee that thou wast naked?
And God asked. me the woman You gave. the woman
me. I don't mind that version. Oh look I screwed up.

call it a garden I wouldn't. nothing floral was there. Sorry
that should be, Was nothing floral there. on my socks
Dressage horses leapt and trotted. messed up I. am
sorry Look I. have rushed to the same mistake I frequently.

a lonely life you led · which follows which · a lonely life
you left · for me · me for · which precedes which · a lonely life
you led a little life you lived a little life alone in a hallway
before me you lived

from *The Rusty Toque*

SONNET L'ABBÉ ℭℬ

CII

My love is intersectional, aware of things white women don't live and men don't go through. More weak I, brown girl, might seem, because my emotions range. Emotional overseers want emotionless thought; the less colour shows the more enlightened I appear. That emotional oversight is a flesh merchandizer's demeanour, the judge's—whose patriarchal esteem rationalized owning slaves, the owner's—whose tongue pronounced vows then pushed between the legs of his help (who were very well behaved for monkeys). The code of stiff-upper-lip, of exquisite control over weeping, was a New World manner developed in the colonies, but was it plantation whippers or skin-stripped pickers whose emotionless gaze was worth emulating? A man I was sweet on just went wild for this girl's "even temper." Such beatitudes for a white, motherly woman's steady, level-headed ways. When has she ever processed the bodily vomit-repulsion vibes that hate cultivated for my mother's figure? How often has she stuffed down the rising self-defence and stopped sullen her breathpipe like a nigger? Show me the neurons firing, synapses every day signalling notice, notice the ratio of the skins, the unmarked vs. the marked: tag, you're it. Run, defencelessness, run! Isn't life more pleasant now than when the nigger's mournful hymns did hush the night, than when brutality tamed that wild music by stringing up runaway threats like skins on every bough? That woman's administrative sweetness is grown on common decency. Only some humans calibrated their demeanour to defer to enlightened- and defend against alt-whites. In the real forum of flesh, unlike here, I sometimes hold my tongue, because I would not tempt the decorum bully's prosecution with my song.

from *Prism*

SOUVANKHAM THAMMAVONGSA ❧

Clown

He was standing at the corner with all his blown-up balloons

He made shapes out of the air and no one understood what it was for

He held these out to anyone who would take them and said they were animals or flowers, his heart

He had spent years training for this moment on the corner handing out nothing

His big bright red shoes glowed like his hair and eyes and mouth

He wanted us to stop and listen and look at what he made and be his friend

He insisted what he made was art

We had all loved this clown once before and joined his brand of entertainment

We saw what he looked like without all that make-up, the prop, the candy

I love you, he said, and we filed out of our houses and filled up the city for him

We alone understood what he made

We were there when the rooms filled with the friends he wanted

We were there before you were, before you knew you could win

And when I quit and spun to split the green bottles spinning he turned and disappeared

A clown is a clown and will always go back to being a clown

It is the sadness of his calling, the joke and code of his ethic

from *The Rusty Toque*

ARLEEN PARÉ ✂

Come the Ungulate

after Steve Collis' "Come the Revolution" from To the Barricades

Come the ungulate   through the streets   the gates   come the deer
they will   on sidewalks small groupings   come the doe and the fawn
families   come the buck   through the streets as if there were none   they
will   complicate   five or six   they thread through   across   ignoring
the cross   they will   intersections   three fawn   behind   they will on
the diagonal   stop signs or stop lights   come the deer   they will at their
own   at the gates   ungulate   they will regal   their pace   they will
slow   through cars   they will   from the north   they come   problemate
laneways   they will roads   into backyards   front yards   they will
graveyards   in the southern direction   as if   preferring the young tops
of short trees   miniatures   pear trees and cherry   they will   over fences
arrive they will   come the tulips   prefer   they will yellow and red   they
will recline   the cemetery is two hundred years old   they will   overlooking
the ocean   they will   range   until the ocean   lie down   as if no one
lounge between headstones   they are not ready to die   three buck they will
ruminate   consume   come the deer   out of campuses and government
gardens   come the deer   come the people   the love   come the hate
they will
            come   the night   under street lamps they weave   come the
park   they will bend their dark shadowed necks under spliced overhead
light   three deer on the grass in the night gardens and hedges   antlers
charcoal grey   navy blue   they will   they could be three oversized hounds
under the broken beam   stillness below the 3 am   the window   they will
paying no attention   as if no populace   no houses   they will   their land
come the doe   buck   come the fawn   come cougar   hunger   come
evening   the night

from *The Malahat Review*

AISHA SASHA JOHN ⚬

CONDITIONS OF ENGAGEMENT

THE LIE YOU TOLD YOURSELF THE RELATIONSHIP REVEALING

YOUR CLOSED HEART'S SUFFERING

THE WIND YOU PUT IN OUR REST

A BEAUTIFUL DULL NAIL CLIPPER

BETWEEN HOW EASY AND GOOD IT IS

THAT'S WHY THERE IS A DOLPHIN ON YOUR KEYCHAIN

WHO LOOKS STUPID AND I LIKED THAT

A DOLPHIN WHO APPEARS TO BE LEARNING

CHANGING POSITIONS IN RELATION TO THE INFORMATION'S
RECEPTION

UNCOMFORTABLE

RECOGNIZING A FEELING AS DISCOMFORT

THE EMOTIONAL INTENSITY OF DYSFUNCTION BULLYING THE
AWKWARDNESS OF ACTUAL INTIMACY

WHO BELIEVES IN ARCHIMEDES?

FASTER AND TENDERERER AND STUFF

DO YOU BELIEVE PEOPLE? I DON'T

AND OBSERVE HOW THEIR BODIES REACT TO WHAT THEY'RE
SAYING

HORSE TRUTH, TEETH

DONKEY TRUTH, SLOW

MALLARD DUCK

THE AGE IS IN YOUR HANDS

I DON'T WANT TO EAT A SPOONFUL OF CRUNCHY ORGANIC PEANUT BUTTER AGAIN

ICE CREAM

UNRIPE PLUM ANYWAY

LOGIC OF NAMING SOMETHING SOMETHING NEGATIVE

WHEN I USED TO SEE YOUR BIG-ASS HEAD ON COLLEGE STREET

I BELIEVE I THINK YOU ADDRESSED ME

I BELIEVE I THINK YOU THINK US INTERLOCUTABLE

LANGUAGE I BELIEVE I THINK YOU THINK WE SHARE

STANDING UP AND THEN SQUATTING

GUESS I'M IN LOVE WITH MY HOBBIES TIMES A FRILLION

I FIGURED OUT WHAT TO DO WITH EVENINGS EITHER SMOKE POT OR DON'T SMOKE POT

IS EVERYBODY LIKE ME UNACTUALIZED OR AM I THE ONLY ONE

IS EVERYONE LIKE ME LIKE IS EVERYONE LIKE BASICALLY ONE PERSON WITH DIFFERENT PARTS AND TIMES

IS THERE ONLY ONE PERSON TIMES VARIATION

FUCKING THE TIME AND TELLING

WARP AND HOW

WHEN YOU WHY

MACKDALICIOUS

IF ONLY IF ONLY IF...OK

from *NewPoetry*

CHRISTOPHER TUBBS ⊗

Customs Declaration to a White Empire

The traveller declares that his name is a silence as dangerous as the river in winter.

The traveller declares that his home address is unpronounceable to most missionaries.

The traveller arrives by air, in the red mists of dread sacrifice; by rail, with the nameless sons of seven generations at his heels; by marine, in a war canoe decked against the flatteries of the champagne socialist; and by highway, trailing tears and stumbling over murdered women.

The traveller declares that the purpose of his trip is "Personal."

The traveller arrives from another country and another time, yet also from this country and from this time, and insists that he be recognized at home.

The traveller declares he cannot free himself from duty.

The traveller further declares that he bears the following goods: One (1) fragrant cedar cloak, rose-gold as the dawn, living and austere. Two (2) adzes in jade, terrible and strange, worn with purposeful use. Three (3) planks of pine, sap-stained, punctured, jeweled, richly frosted in otter's teeth and fire-blacked bone. Four (4) blankets, imported and diseased, one sewn into wrappings for a child and another clawed in fear. Five (5) treaty drafts, four unsigned, the fifth edited in treachery and re-notarized by a respected gentleman of leisure at Ottawa. Six (6) memories of mother's glance falling absently on the reflection of the shadow of the great tree, saying, "We'll talk about the reservation when you're older." Seven (7) stillborn half-breed cousins made fertilizer to a schoolyard garden, buried there by a stern father's command and a trowel.

The traveller certifies that his declaration is true, but cannot be complete; memory flows off the table's edge from an over-filled cup and is lost in Christian soil.

from *The Capilano Review*

JOHN PASS ✿

Deer

Waiting for anything new about deer.
Waiting for everything known about deer.
Waiting for a path to open through the underbrush

stranded here species of watchful waiting, soft-
bodied, straddling salal inside

invisibly pixellated environs (densely specific loci
of alertness) who might stride gingerly off or

leap into your swerve. Sinew and twitch and stilted
stepping is our signature through browse, through ponder,

through what's left of your garden, your uneventful
drive home. Who would carry work-gloves

to drag the famous corpse/trope to the shoulder
of yet another North American poem, or returning
in them and an old jacket find only smears

of snot and blood on the asphalt? Who'd get lucky
in the interim, tossing the venison into their pulled-over
pick-up? Not us. First time walking the land we'd asked
the realtor (of all people) re the pressed moss hollows

below the bluff (she) *do deer sleep here? And*
(me) *would these be good places*
for the well?

It's aquifer not ground-
water, drilled to through granite you want
with the head near the house ... The springy

(still hanging) first question's still dreaming
still pressing dimensions of presence, succulent
destinations: sapling in the pre-dawn, patio shade

under climber roses, caged peas. Statuesque, testing
the breeze up the driveway, or in the orchard a

low-limbed leaf-cluster in a fore-limbed
up-pawing hoof-scrabble and   stretch, it listens.

from *Prairie Fire*

ROBIN RICHARDSON ✂

Disembodied at the Botanical Gardens

Could be a raven, humiliation of, a wife.
Or better: koi, albino in that garden
where a bridge arcs like two arms joined
hand-to-wrist or fern-to-lookout to a kid

who stops to add me to his catalogue
of reasons to exist. The corridor of cherry
blossoms laced with little girls in Vogue-
appropriate attire makes a pink so sweet

it's hard to swallow. Could be the effigy:
life-like, dwarfed by ferns, drawn by boys
with Asperger's and aptitudes in line
to be unearthed. Maybe my face will be

what clicks: some shy savant who finds
his gift. There is a word for stuck in form.
Please let me be a blaze. I will destroy,
I mean create again this place.

from *The Puritan*

CANISIA LUBRIN ✂

Final Prayer in the Cathedral of the Immaculate Conception II

In the end
we'd settle on paraphrase

Tongues prostrate, still, like sages
after a lifetime of silence

With our names abandoned in
the weight of our diviners

Our serial practice of voice
the unthinking

deep within us,
crescendos through space

ornaments in place of moon
and air

everywhere,
coming like a dawn, withheld

bursting, we descend
with the countdown of our rebirth

with the return of early spring birds
littering the sky, we

water, hunting ourselves *through*
a rare falling

—are prepared to know our defence,
keeping it locked when we have no use for it

how, at first, coming home to crayon'd walls,
strokes of pure spirit and bone of the ones
who drew them, now absent, makes us

mad. What we ought to have heard
in the warring voices fleeing the night
as we carried on our fleeting fall—

was the half-rumoured lilt of thunder
in the baby's cry demanding plot
and reasons bigger than the guns
that stole us into a twilight we struggle
to understand.

—Ancient sages might have
spoken that same hyperkiller language
of dilating cervixes:

Labour is the early war, the one less feared
whose vaporous monotones of sorrow disappear too soon

And mothers—already overburdened by the fallout taxes of
some distant relative's original sin,
in which free will was enacted and land was spared
and bestowed by a God wise enough to
keep distance between earth and sky

—ask: who's duty now it is
to shed the need for things to come to blow?

That baldheaded anomaly in the
vulva's hoist

packing up its mallets, beating its sandals
one-handed, breaking tears as it enters the world

whose flaking skin is the utopist shade of the galaxy…

And who cares for these fables that console
but not enough

when the room half full of cobaltous children
when the age of the singing bowl
when the puppetry, fugues of string
and votive, withhold warmth only long
enough for us to clock our times

and return home. To the bad seeds
who've sucked up nicknames like
bandit and *colt* and *cockman,*
germinated from their toddling days
in company of small hulks and rubber giraffes
like secrets packed away in the attic

These are the children
we tell bedtime stories
of our undying
love
of the silhouettes.

So while we go on and limit sorrow to money and arms,
that knock-of-the-sill and conscience, blanking
the source of our ebbing genealogies,

our anthologized dead
still touch everything,

numbering the stars and known universe
as we find ourselves still prostrate beneath
a sun still raging, before any of us even break
into the work of our absence in the memorial,

we have been conquered,
fingers still jagged from battle,
and we go on
and we age
into nocturne.

from *The Rusty Toque*

TIM BOWLING ❧

Found Poem of Strait of Georgia Insults

You're a Dull Oregon grape you black-bellied plover of a long-billed
dowitcher. You lugworm you screwshell. What a walleye pollock of a Kelp-
encrusting Bryozoan. Yeah, you heard me, you Suborbicular kellyclam
Twelve-tentacled parasitic anemone. Your scaup's always been Lesser you
three-spine stickleback Spring-headed sea squirt. That's right, you Hairy
chiton, I said it. Don't give me any of your Green falsejingle, you Fat gaper.
Who do you think you are, the Lord dwarf-venus himself? You're nothing
but a Flap-tip piddock with an Aggregated nipple sponge. Come on, you
Pile worm you Dubious dorid you squat lobster. You want a piece of me?
Agh, you're all Hollow green nori you yellowleg pandalid. I wouldn't waste
my time on a solitary tunicate like you. Yeah, so's your mother you Oblique
yoldia. Goddamned mud shrimp. Surf scoter. Sea-clown triopha. Gribble.
Sea noodle. Dunce cap limpet. Bladderclam. Whelk.

from *The Malahat Review*

SACHIKO MURAKAMI ⁓

Good God/Bad God

HONESTY
I try to sneak my god in, which obviously won't work. She is not a sneaky god.

REGRET
My dead father acquires a god. The only evidence of their relationship is the backyard full of shit.

RESPONSIBILITY
I am to take out someone else's god for a walk, and someone else's child from school. I wander off on a journey, alone.

FEAR
On retreat in the country, the locals and their gods mock me and my god. We barricade ourselves against their threats.

RAGE
Near a sidewalk crowded with god walkers, I am stuck in a car with my angry, unleashed god.

LOVE
Some young gods fit in the palm of your hand. Some have definite heft. All are cared for by someone else.

INTELLIGENCE
My god is prone to attacking children. We walk with purpose into a schoolyard.

SHAME
I take my god to an improbable park. She finds the only mud puddle and rolls in it.

REDEMPTION
My dead god is waiting for me, near the pool.

from *NewPoetry*

DAPHNE MARLATT ✂

l'heure bleue

below freezing warm red mist off Astoria's all-night sign
cut by house roofs here one bright back porch two rooms aglow
alley   dark bulk of mountains   apparition snow   halflit

here, here
                    atmospheric scattering of the not-yet

can't find my way back to monsoon heat with S who walks faster
through Chulia Street's motor bike zip by parked cars   cement
blocks dodgy underfoot tiled walkways crammed bike-by-rattan
seat grey husky chained to a platform backpackers chat up resident
eaters snack at white kopi or kedai or cappuccino she's looking for
bee hoon me for char kway teow

so we get to the padang's white colonial government porticoes
seat of state and static rain trees lift dark crowns to fading
light it's rainbow drift as if from sea level some mystique
through horizon light the trees the esplanade *en flot* oh

a man blowing
                    bubbles for kids'
                              outstretched fingers reach

                                        pffft and gone

from *The Capilano Review*

BREN SIMMERS ☙

If Spring

If rollercoaster flocks of bushtits
and golden-crowned kinglets.
If insects tap morse code on glass.
If snowmelt, if flood warning.
If icebergs calve inside ribs.
If alevins hidden in river gravel,
button up their yolk sacs.
If kingfishers pluck parr marks.
If we crack our exoskeltons and emerge
with compound eyes, winged?
If we push against our limits
to redraw them. If daylight stalks
both dawn and dusk.
If daffodils shear soil crusts.
If elderberries sprout breast buds.
If seed catalogues trump
playoff 'staches. If alder catkins
blush red. If cotton sheets,
if coatless. If we dwell again
in the conditional.
If, when.

from *The Malahat Review*

SELINA BOAN ❦

inside the vein:

"our bodies are our libraries— fully referenced in memory, an endless resource, a giant database of stories" —Monique Mojica

this is you, and her, and him—   the story of moss tip toeing its way along the underbelly of a bridge, river eyes like the crack of fat when a hide is peeled away, taste of elk—raw and soft in your teeth at easter dinner, pop of blood running on your plate, this is the half story of a boy, a man, a father who was tripped, round-lipped stumble a stream (a run, a burn, a beck), the ground and the getting up again, nuns marching across a field in the snow with their forgiveness and their stew, a girl, a woman, a mother raising, this is you daughter, and all your quiet wants and none of your knowing, a feeling that wants to stick to the skin but can't quite remember how, rock, paper, river, you girl are a gamble made during the planting of trees, a pickup truck and a bump of plastic beads stitched by hand, a clot of years you don't know how to carry and the fear that this body is not where you belong

"For a people who have had much of their knowledge of the past severed, blood memory promises a direct link to the lives of our ancestors" —Bonita Lawrence

from *Contemporary Verse 2*

*The line "rock paper river" comes from the name of artist Faye HeavyShield's 2005 art exhibition at Gallery Connexion, Fredericton, New Brunswick.

MEREDITH QUARTERMAIN ❧

Letter to bp on Train Crossing the Rockies

Notation
in the landscape of a nation,
you wrote, Oh Horseman,
baggage cars rolling along St. Eel,
"where is this poem going"
to raddle the maintrains
and dead reckon?

Moose Lake: Poet notes pickup truck,
motorboat, black and white signs bearing names.
Bear. *Au côté gauche.* Bare crumbling marker
au côté gauche. Bare heaving sea-bottoms
weathered layers.

Who will bear us?
CN English. CN Devona. CN Dalehurst.
Threading wires this to that. Swan Landing.
Les montagnes, les ours forbearance
in England's masquerade of names
for Cree land with young trees,
land jutting in water, land of mortal men,
land of ponds, land she lives on,
land open.

Welcome to Alberta,
factoid bartender booms.

Queen Victoria's daughter
has thirty-five species of fish,
one thousand five hundred species of plants:
Hinton Chrysler.
Hinton Motel. Stetson Hinton.
Hinton Arby's. Hinton Rexall.
Hinton Timberland, Liquor Store, ReMax.

Flat hills. Flatter.
Flatten. Flattening
who who who
dollars to docents to frankincense.
Accents to nuisance.
Dissents to reticence.

from *Prism*

GEORGE ELLIOTT CLARKE ଔ

Lincoln Plans for Peace (*Pace* Appomattox)

Aprilis cometh—
unanimous melt-water streaming
under the Capitol's bridges
reaming Washington's ravines—

following the horrible, endless January—
those two faces glancing backward and forward
at *Hell*—
the tornado *chiaroscuro* that is *War*—

contention of lead, steel, iron, fire—
and damnation of the flesh—
its bleeding ruination.
I so do want to savour

orchards trembling under rain water.
So many good people have perished
due to good aim
and good metal of adversaries.

Battlefields' muddy soils—
churned, baptized, by piss, blood, tears—
host Union bodies,
I'd like cast in gold.

Every corpse has a face like beaten earth
or pressed-down snow.
        The *Constitution* is, in truth,
a whites-only song,

the spouts of breath
of our Union boys,
plus the answering Southern shouting.
The road to Appomattox

was a cloud of iron—
flame spurt, blood spurt.

Earthworms cut the dead—
painlessly—

to pieces.
Lee came at me—
on behalf of Davis—
a lot of frisky galloping

plus black-soil massacres,
totting up to 500,000;
each Virginia field—
after the crimson binge—

floods wholly violet.
The dead know verminous caresses:
Flies gobbling up the gore.
In *War*, a victor can't be sluggish

at *Slaughter*.
His Conscience is his molars.
A martial president couples *Cruelty*
and *Theology*:

A just God desecrates our enemies.
I know these truths....
Damn! Even Gettysburg is now
a battalion of flowers,

after the wine-red bleating
of the bayonet-defeated,
their salutations to mosquitoes;
after the junkyard-dog ferocity

of contending "cousins"....
Magnolia offers a serene stink.
I look out over cratered fields—
still as sunny as America—

and I spy, finally liberated,
a rustic, imitation Africa—
a flourish of melanin
among unspoiled dew.

I hear the Negroes—
each brazen throat—
the puce cackles that stir us all.
Their "spirituals" sound *romanceros**—

the anthems of a people
poorly suited to *Caution,*
who have *Liberty* mixed with their blood.
Bullets no longer flute from guns.

I'm the big-shot *blanco*—
no toothless, Head-of-State—
who made the South undertake
a gross inventory of corpses

under a falling roof of crows.
Bronze statues and cannon brood
on this fire-shattered Republic;
yet, I feel Mozart-exuberant.

True: I dreamt recently
I was a lamentable cadaver
in an amenable coffin.
But no *Butchery* is decorous..

[Frankfurt (Germany) 26 *juin* mmxiii]

from *Contemporary Verse 2*

*Spanish: Ballads

SHARRON PROULX-TURNER ❧

the longhouse

> *there are people who will try to hurt you because of the good they see in you, needing that good for themselves. they'll try to beat it out of you. when you come to know that, don't become like those people.*
> —evelyn t.r. boyce

I dream of a large room, where the wind blowing indoors doesn't seem out of the ordinary. though the room is full of people, I feel alone, lonely for a friend. my childhood home was like that, like I didn't belong, with my mom stretching out a silence I wasn't meant to break. the silence concerned me, mom teaching the older ones, the younger ones the dangers of me. my biggest flaw was I was too nice, too kind. not natural, my mom would say. born evil, that one. watch your back.

in dreamworld there are mirrors up above in the large room. I can see myself and each strand of my hair contains volumes of knowledge forming along the waves. the wind picks up words, like dust from my hands, my skin, my hair—swirling them into a tiny twister whose point reaches into my left eye. and rather than close my eyes, I hold them open to the harshness of those words, the blinding sting that opens a doorway to the past.

I'm reminded of a story I heard some years ago, where trickster loses her eyes after juggling them for too long—even though she's warned this will happen—and her eyes don't return. she starts to go around with flowers in her empty sockets, telling the people she encounters how special her eyes are and how she can see things no one else can see. person after person offers to trade one eye for one of hers, until, one day, a girl offers to trade both her eyes for these special eyes that can see things no one else can see. when the trade is made, the girl is left without sight.

but the girl knows that darkness holds stories and songs of great power, and when she recounts them in her mind, they shift her thoughts away from herself to the voices of the women who came before her.

she dreams about her grandmother. in the dream, she's a teen and there are other kids, lots of them, maybe sisters and brothers and cousins. her grandmother has them all helping to clear out a canoe, a very, very long canoe that's large enough for an extended family. the canoe is made from bark, not from wood. because she's the oldest, her grandmother asks her to go out with the canoe and retrieve a medicine from the bottom of the water. the water is dark and murky. it takes several dives before the girl is able to pull up the medicine for her grandmother. she knows this is a powerful healing medicine. when she reaches the surface after her final dive and opens her eyes, she's in a circle of women.

she goes around the circle shaking the women's hands, introducing herself. she reaches her mother, surprised she's there. when they shake hands, they laugh and shake hands again. her mother's hand feels like her own hand, like she's shaking her own hand. her mother's talking and the girl leans down to hear what her mother is saying, her left ear to her mother's mouth. her mother makes a joke in her ear. the girl tells a joke back. wakes herself up laughing.

from *Canadian Literature*

BILLY-RAY BELCOURT ❧

Love is a Moontime Teaching

love is a moontime teaching
is your kookum's crooked smile when you pick up the phone
is another word for body
body is another word for campfire smoke
campfire smoke is the smell he leaves behind in your bed sheets after the
    breakup
the word for hate sex is forest
forest sometimes means hope or lonely (depends on who you ask)
lonely is a movie called *taxi zum klo* about white gay men who risk tiptoeing
    through desire's
minefields for ten minutes of something better than living
living is going to bingo to pay the bills after you quit your job that barely
    paid the bills
paying the bills is sometimes a metaphor for cancer
cancer is a diagnosis handed down to an 18-year-old girl from the rez
the rez is another word for body
the body is a myth
is the only good news the doctor gives you when your cells run amok
amok is the border that the skin doesn't remember how to secure anymore
anymore is the feeling you get when a police officer pulls you over because
    he thinks you're driving a stolen vehicle
a stolen vehicle is the nickname you give to love
love is the nickname you give to the hole in the wall from that time your
    cousin's boyfriend punched it
a hole in the wall is what you call the present and the labour it takes to
    survive

from *The Malahat Review*

PHIL HALL ☙

The Lyric

In memoriam Tomas Tranströmer
(1931-2015)

This body   a circular arrow   loosed   spinning   inside a flagstone

ah   as in Hans Arp   an ankle   fits an instep

the high plateaus   unlost   I say unlost   though it's not true

a whistle   of sea lily   powder   in a flying shard   of limestone

ah   as in Hans Arp   an ankle   fits an instep

the sleeping positions   endless

•

Acting crazy
we were stopped
                    by a stand-up bass
    on its side in the pasture

morning   no one else around

The angel who grew inside it   like a snail
has abandoned it   & gravity

cello   viola   lute
each housed a different breed of angel

Don't say   angel   that's stupid

in its burning curiosity
    about E #
                each   *as if*
was willing to volute   wear   & pull   a shell

each drew   its own   inexplicable
now common   dank   trail

Run & find strings

•

To tell what happened to you   is not a poem

there is not enough in the story of your life to make poetry

yet roars   The Lyric
a calamitous wall   by the platform   you wait on

little black freight train   match-sticks   & epoxy
each car full of _____

start your silly lists

archaisms   desperate gerunds   *faux picante*

•

The day Grandmother died
a parcel came for her   no return address

a photo album   with an elk embossed on the cover

snap-shots
          she was accidentally in
throughout her simple life
              She happened
   to be walking by

& two sketches of her
  done in secret by strangers

each wayward image   culled
  from other peoples' photo albums
rummage sales   landfill

a wide hat & a scarf along a ship's rail

thumb-blur   a puffy sleeve   60s glasses

protest marches   wedding deceptions

kids held high   a little bare foot so like an ear   Rare Beach

security   a mirror flash   then lab scans

Tell us the story of each photo

I don't have time   I can't recollect

then she said   laughing   coughing
Arms wide   rush   to meet the parade

we buried her album with her
so no you can't see it

Arms wide   I try to   Gran

like a   like a

•

Now I too   get to hear the cicada   & say so

its no-carapace blues   pierce mine

the phrase   *all the time in the world*   is a pencil sharpener

to squeeze the I'm   out of a word   don't squeeze

are you carrying fervour   or currying favour

the line   with no hook   is my fish

from *Contemporary Verse 2*

DANIEL SCOTT TYSDAL ❧

A MAD Fold-In Poem

A ▶   ◀ B

You—this mucky fire slathered in my mind's frame
—are as committed to me as artists are to art. At times,
your voice is constant—"kill yourself, kill yourself, kill
yourself"—fists punching clay with the aim to make me
nothing more than punched clay. Other times, you're
a cinema in my skull, screening me mangled: one leg
auger-mauled, hand vice-crushed, eye pencil-blinded to life
—"end it," you say, in the scene you loop: this cinema's walls
with a bullet burst. At parties, you shape a sinister play from
others' glances: "hate him," "idiot," "fool." When I bloom,
a sun, all alight and rising, you flatten my lift into lines
on a page like Jaffee's in the back of MAD; you fold it
over and now the rise is the wound from a wing cleaved
and then gilded, the bloom's a thousand-foot fall, the sun
a drain. Yet with each step the unrelenting chorus of you
circles round me, another chorus surfaces to surround you: the
line of sheltering trees artists grow, loamy and ablaze, against
your gale, the melodies of friends whose works asphyxiate your
symphony, the lessons students teach about tipping your
plinths, the magic of bringing nib to page and penning life
with urgency and patience, word by word, with abandon
and care. Even though I know it can never silence you, I love
this inky trick because it fills the blank before you can, marks
up your script, swallows you choking in a page-mutating
fold, so your cruel barks, garbled, almost seem to say:

A ▶   Fold back so "A" meets "B"   ◀ B

from *Poetry*

PEARL PIRIE ❦

Misremembering the Colour of Books,
A Something Something in Canada Where

time refused to pass, created
a quintessential traffic jam
at the intersection of

it & space.

            each waves cordially
but neither wavers

politely muling   .
with a cow's mid-gaze
that the other go first.

behind them
all the dimensions pile
without a swayback of objection

from *Ottawater*

FAIZAL DEEN ☙

Modern Politics

After C.L.R. James

WHAT WE OWE TO ANCIENT GREECE

~~jumbie so deep no broom beat it out me~~   headmaster omitting
~~so deep no pointer broom beat it out me~~   the unspeakable vice of the Greeks
~~no pointer broom dry coconut leaves beat it out me~~   in Uncle Iqbal

HOW DIRECT DEMOCRACY WORKED

pawpaw seed jumbie   the Risk board democracy wins ~~luck~~
~~Pears soap mouth~~   don't play in the masjids after dark
dash this child   ~~Grandma says~~

THE RELATION OF THE GREEK TO HIS GOVERNMENT

~~them fuck make me~~   Gare Centrale daddy
Mom cervix small   warning you,
~~she bleed out~~   ~~stay clear of Greektown~~

GREAT ROME AND LITTLE ATHENS

~~at the Mephistopheles by the glory holes~~   Auntie Moon's punctured
     honeymoon
~~someone white will push me away~~   flames Roman nose ~~Walkman burn~~

ST. JOHN'S VISION OF A HARMONIOUS SOCIETY

~~sea level springtides~~   the fifth monarchy
waves Atlantic   the ~~English~~ think they're Romans
Grandpa's promenade   the ~~Americans~~, too
~~this~~ seawall built by convicts   Uncle Iqbal
~~all that~~ granite on the Mazaruni   ~~sewed his money~~ into suits when he left

THE CITY-STATES OF THE MIDDLE AGES

~~nothing will change~~   old Ilfords from Florence
~~we will swear white~~ like Horatio in the masjids   in Grade 5 you show off

THE BIRTH OF PARLIAMENTARY DEMOCRACY

Main Street monkeypod trees   ~~the queen~~ riding high on ~~her king~~ hard
afternoon crotons cattleyas clusters   the Persauds on Bridge Street ~~are protestants~~
two centuries of Guyana   ~~not as good at business, Grandpa says~~

CROMWELL AND THE LEVELLERS

~~prayers I can't pronounce~~   Richard Harris alone with Mom at the Plaza
bizmAllah? hiruvman? niraheem?   ~~who will insist first~~
Georgetown, Venice of the West Indies   ~~on the profits of language~~

THE BEGINNING OF MODERN PHILOSOPHY

Hesperus ~~shoulder this history~~   ecrasez l'infame Uncle Ken
~~him ships bottle me heart~~   walking through Mourne Jaloux
wide coolie Victoria lilies   after Ronald Reagan's "~~gnat~~"

THE AGE OF REASON

Kali coming to life behind Sinbad   ~~what you've written before~~ in this age of reason
an Ottawa special effect: "~~see, Orientalist!, see?~~"   my hands have grown insane

ROUSSEAU REJECTS PURE REASON

~~the seas swell up/the catfish sing~~   in Mom's shaky camera

HE REPUDIATES REPRESENTATIVE GOVERNMENT

British Guiana ~~in~~ 1831   Walter Rodney at war ~~with~~
~~I can't forget that~~   the people who rob their generations of jungle

WHAT CAN REPLACE REPRESENTATIVE GOVERNMENT

~~"I cross dark water, too"~~   Auntie Zeedy ~~cutting off your hair to make you look~~
~~"I cross dark water with~~ the Hindoos"   more like a boy in the eyes of an
abstract God

from *Ottawater*

WAASEYAA'SIN CHRISTINE SY ✧

my umbilical cord, map trail seasonal camp: a poetics of work

i.

identity indigenous   negative + positive sculpted scoops of authenticity
+ fake-ness. shards of chert deftly nicked away leaving a bundle of flakes,
impressions, and

a (finely) crafted tool. a sharp round tool: sharp for cutting into + garnering
life; round smooth parts my organs. ode (oh-day). my heart, n'ode.

ii.

some of us were getting on about (inauthentic) indigenous identity claims
and their close relative, *performing indigenous*. conclusion: repairing from
colonial forces is a real verb; so too is industry.   in this climate, even
i with my phenotype, kinship ties, and relational knowledges, take the
questions and disclose long-winded, beautiful story over again. none of us
are above the requirements of the new world yet many of us expect a pass.

                    how are you how you are?

some of the established wag their fingers at holding others to account
for their claims and performances (because ~~friendship~~ power relations)
while others who live just real native poor ponder why some get the space,
resources, and opportunities. i don't know if this difference between
resources is traditional for anishinaabe or a modern product of colonial
capitalism + marketability. i don't know what it means.

i pack Gregory Scofield's medicine wisdom deeply into my chest. it beats
simpatico with my heart. a cradling. a rhythmic caress and pat. it allows me
to formulate convoluted thoughts: if you are going to be in the enlightened
world as indigenous, and be the beneficiary of places and relations where
enlightenment lives, then at least step too into the shadow and tell us about
the hard work, the precariousness, the fragility of re-relationing kinship ties,
mistakes made. tell us about your privileges.

tell us the pain of be(com)ing indigenous.

i mean really,

don't tell us a story,

tell us your story,
storyteller.

iii.

here is a story of empty + hungry.

in one version, they *extract from* and *take on* the being of those with whom
they engage in relationship-kahn.   kahn is an anishinaabe suffix
sounding like *con* and meaning *fake*.

i shit you not.

they siphon from the workpassiontalentgenerositybeing of others and with
some tweaking present it as though their own. they do it well. swooners
swoon. still hungry, they continue eating the long hard heart work of others.
they see a story they want and go after it. nomnomnom. windigo feast.

in another version, empty + hungry enters liminal spaces. is heart-y. hesitant,
like entering into ceremony. hunker down for the long haul of relational
reciprocity.

> all the g(l)ory bits?
> yes.
> all the g(l)ory bits, too.

presenting only two versions of a story is a dichotomy. limited. hugely
problematic.   still, a dichotomy is an effective tool for wrenching out big
truths.   finely crafted tools are for the nuancing.

iv.

here are the nuances of my be(com)ing indigenous:
        1) cut open chest to expose n'ode
        2) follow n'ode
        3) honour gut & intuition
        4) speak/do from a place of hard earned western +

anishinaabe education, ancestral intellect drawn from my anishinaabe mother and my white father, and self-respect

     5) put my asemaa down + plant clearly articulated seeds

     6) wait wait wait to not be broke + simultaneously call the money to come my way, come my way, come my way. (in a capitalist world, relationing costs money. gas money. food money. tool-getting money. license money. driving money. gifting money. wood money. clothes money. every be(com)ing indigenous knows this.)

     7) on a borrowed dime, keep storying

v.

where i live as visitor, power is exchanged ceremonially, out in the open, in the form of quarters. there is the Lord and there are Crosses. there is a facing to the east and a reverence for the exposed earthen floor and open fire. here, it is all about ode. i'm in relationships with people with whom i can discuss all these things. friendship. i didn't even have to make a request with asemaa (tobacco) this time.

standing here, facing home :: east, i retrace baby steps and the long road. i chuckle; Alanis Morissette looks like some indigenous people i know and her website entitled after herself shows that she appropriates dream catchers and antlers but still, her song resonates: isn't it ironic   the trail towards my future is marked with place and relational bundles longed for all my life. it was only on driving towards them in anticipation of driving by that i was able to pick them up for the first time. these bundles, generously shared, make the travelling light and i am reminded of another story of re-sibling-ing....

materiality + memory. i am homesick for the future.

vi.

home is a map, trails, and seasonal camps; map, trails, and seasonal camps, my umbilical cord. if you were to sit atop a satellite orbiting Turtle Island, maintain your balance and zoom in, you would see the way biological and cultural yearnings for anishinaabe life form a long, windy, flesh-coloured trail around gichi gamigoong (the Great Lakes) with one long standard deviation to the west. there are places where this trail bunches up, circles, encircles itself—an animal making a concave wow in the earth getting ready to hunker down, rest.

vii.

here is a quasi-final ending to this story. my placenta,
umbilical cord, and heart are all over gichi gamingoong
but the quasi-final ending to this story
is a dot on a map called Canada,
representing a place called Sioux Lookout.

Sioux Lookout is in Ontario.
Northwestern Ontario.

Sioux Lookout has a settler history.

it has an oral history, too. An anishinaabe oral history. A "this-is-the-story-
my-aunts-who-i-just-met-told-me-whilst-visiting-for-the-first-time-on-my-
way-out-west" story. It goes like:

> We'll take a drive later so you can meet your cousin before he goes to
> work. I want you to see the lake and the mountain, too.
>
> That there is the lake and the mountain. This was our families'
> traditional trapping grounds. That there end of the lake is where we
> used to play.

i remember that.

this is living oral history being told in an SUV alongside a public beach in
downtown-ish Sioux Lookout.

there is also a bend in a river ways-away from the settler occupied trapping
grounds that my cousin showed me as we were getting ready to go out on
the water. the sun was shining bright and reflecting shiny off the tall waving
grasses making it hard to see the shoreline but he pointed,

> There. That's where your great grandmother lived. she had a cabin
> there. I remember we'd go visit her from the school at Pelican.

this is recent living oral history.

in 1997 one of my white brothers died and two weeks later my anishinaabe
brother emerged by way of dream and a friend's aunt's quirky habit of

reading personal ads. through him—my second anishinaabe relative after my mother—I met my third anishinaabe relative, an aunt. through her, during an afternoon visit, I learned that she, my mother, and their sister were stolen away to Pelican Falls residential school three times. They kept running away back up the trap line to their stepfather and on the third time, the RCMP left them alone. this is less-recent living oral history about three anishinaabe girls. Northern Ontario beats like a heart on living oral histories about anishinaabe, cree, and métis girls. let's be sure that the good heart and talentedly crafted stories that iijkiiwenyag (friends) Gord Downie-baa and Joseph Boyden tell about one boy don't serve as replacement for everyone's stories. let's be sure that our families keep our stories alive for ourselves.   ourselves. in all time and space dimensions. not just the present.

viii.

the work of be(com)ing indigenous is hard work.

this is not a poem.
this is not an award nomination.
it is not a contest submission.

this is not a haunting.
this is neither obituary nor personal legacy.
it is not a smudge, sweatlodge, or shaking tent.

this is the poetics of *one* umbilical cord unburying anishinaabe country.
it's oral history alive + living for the future.

from *Contemporary Verse 2*

ANNE MARIE TODKILL ✿

November, Stormont County

1
Hawk month. Glint-light slant;
clouds smudged mauve. The fields
like salt-prints, tarnished. Corn sere
or stubbled. Burn-piles flare vermilion;
smoke stretches leeward, low.
Backhoes pause beside trenched earth,
black spools of drainage pipe.
As if silent, a train from Montreal.

2
Keep one eye on traffic, the other
on roadside trees, until you see
a bleb in dry branches that is not
the empty hive of paper wasps,
a squirrel pod, curled porcupine,
or plastic bag snagged by wind,
but a red-tail hunkered above ditches,
waiting for a signal: vole.
Voler.
You'll never match that readiness.
In a moment you'll mistake
five hundred buntings landing
for a skiff of snow.

3
Incoming, they materialize from fifty thousand
vanishing points, crystals on pollen: snow geese,
blizzarding the sewage lagoon, landfill, shaved field,
impromptu truckstop on the flyway, stirring unrest,
eruptions, the usual brawls, off-pitch honking, flashing
their gang insignia (black on the wingtip, very sharp)
signalling likeness, signalling kind, signalling swoop,
assemble, flockflockflock, swirl, assemble, break it up;
heliographing nownownow and almost, almost; flagging
traffic into lines, a chromosome-crossing, X and Y,
breaking and repairing until the glyph appears,

aerodynamic letterform for followfollowfollow,
and each bird, lifting, recedes to a cypher,
wingbellywing, species code,
blackwhiteblack marker,
shimmering particle,
DNA.

from *The New Quarterly*

SARAH TOLMIE ଔ

On Seeing an Ad for Vaginal Rejuvenation in *Grand Magazine*

I had already reached the thought
I should write about my twat
Independently.

In Old French there are quite a lot
Of poems in which twats speak
Eloquently.

I had been going to say
Perimenopausally
Alas for me

That every period's become an elegy.
Unlike in my twenties, say
When each one passed

Triumphally, and I raised a glass
To being unencumbered.
Now each hot flash whispers to me

My days are numbered
No longer by twenty-eight
But other sums:

How much I weigh, how much I make.
How much to rejuvenate
My kitchen or my cunt?

These home magazines are blunt
About updating tiles, faucets, patios;
The care of our breasts and cuticles,

Real or applied.
The target audience is fifty-five,
Too old to muse about another child.

Except the men, but what they need
They can find online.
Magazines exist to serve women's appetites.

The sacred topic of fertility
Among the late-blooming middle class
Is glossed over entirely.

All the treatments that we've had, and all the twins
And each near miss are not discussed in venues such as this.
Yet our vaginas persist unto this last.

They even get a full page spread.
We can shore up their lisping mouths
After all the things they've said.

from *The New Quarterly*

CATRIONA WRIGHT ℭℨ

Origin Story

Some of it was probably cozy and nice. Close to the fire,
silly drunk on sweet fermented plums. Some of it was urgent.

One last romp before the man strapped on his sandals
and dragged his sword into a bloody field. And some quiet,

unbuttoning all those pearl buttons from nape
to feet, folding calf-length velvet breeches before slipping

into cold starch. It's unclear how much cunnilingus went on.
I'm guessing no diamante nipple clamps, but I could be wrong.

Some kinky stuff went down, for sure, maybe involving butter churns.
I don't know. Mammoth tusks? Some people are super brave and creative.

Poems about fleas and dire prophecies and pushy parents
and help with milking and mercy were all possible motives

as were cute overbites and obedience and hunger
and wide birthing hips and relentless seasick nights.

Some of it happened inside a marriage and some outside
and some between enemies in a burning village.

Maybe not all of it was consensual. Let's be honest, history is cruel.
Some women limped out of it, tried to ignore the shame

swelling their bellies. Some women resigned themselves,
just waited for it to end, floating above their bodies.

Some of the women would rather have done it with other women.
Some of the men would rather have been women.

Some couplings were just right, whispering nothings,
mapping mole constellations, all moans and giddy filth.

Back then it couldn't be as clean and deliberate. No thawed vials
of specimen, no donor profiles, no eggs suspended in gel.

Just so many bodies crashing into each other, standing, sitting,
on knees, on beds, with oak bark gnarls pressing

into sweaty backs, with straw in hair, with sand grinding
against hands, with goose down pillowing heads,

the smell of whale oil and opium, of elk velvet, of roast hare,
of piss and mead and beeswax, of coal smoke and manure,

so much skin and so many promises, such love and pain
and contempt and doubt, such hope and duty, all that fucking

creating and creating and creating and creating
you

from *Lemon Hound*

ERIN NOTEBOOM ❧

Pavlovsk Station

Outside of Leningrad, digging up potatoes,
are scientists. It is 1941. The Germans closing in.
The scientists, men and women, are from Pavlovsk Station.
Their work is to save the six thousand kinds
of potatoes, the banks of edible seeds in glassine packets,
the two hundred varieties
of cherry. It will not be easy.
There are rats, and even rats
are not the hungriest.
There is bread made of sawdust.
Jam made of wallpaper. For 872 days,
Leningrad folds inward like a fertilized flower.
640,000 dead, and mostly of starvation—but these
are merely numbers. Here is the heart
of science: in the basement, the man in charge of rice
starves to death, while leaning on the sacks of rice.

from *Prism*

SUE GOYETTE ❧

from Penelope

I wake to a horse. Are you in my dream? I'm asked.
Do I look like a dream? I reply. Were we just pillaging

a castle but didn't take the gold? I'm asked. I would never
take anyone else's gold, I reply. Was there a goddess

who spoke as an owl, commanding us to leave
by way of the river? I'm asked. Was she wearing a long string

of pearls under her breasts? I reply. Are you the lady
who's been waiting for a husband for a pathetically long time?

I'm asked. Are you fucking kidding me? I reply. The horse
and I study each other until our edges meld, our forces join.

*

I wake to watch us. What did you do to your hair? we ask.
Our hands fledging, aloft. Nothing, we reply.

Is this the marsh of another dream or us reacquainting with the next
vow? If Odysseus is a mast, am I now a stalk, flowering?

We negotiate the distance between us with awkwardness.
When I tell him of the small hosts of lichen and my sips,

he tastes them. When he speaks the names of his lost men, I hold them
on my tongue until the names wear out their chiming. And when Telemachus

weeps a boy for each year his father has been gone, we open our arms
to welcome them. So many small boys clamouring for family.

from *Lemon Hound*

DANI COUTURE ∝

Pioneer 14

Addendum to the pudendal cleft rubbed
off, out, or plaqued shut with gold. Our god,
one of them, magic-tricked a woman
from bone.

　　We call this humour.

As part of a codicil, should vandals—interstellar
dust or key—scratch a fissure, a recording will play.

　　A cosmic Easter egg.

A bartender in Wilmington who remarked
salsa dancers make the best guests. Impossible
to tell if there are twenty or ten in the room
once attached. It has been said we are best
and worst when organized.

Jet propulsion will eventually erupt
and cause a break between her legs,
at which point she will take off.

The man's ninth finger, his cardinal
rose, will orient you to Earth.

His breasts are lacking, but do not point it out.
We call them *pecs*. His nipples are seeds
birds feed on. We have birds. Do you?

　　Are you?

Women have nipples, which
are shown, but may not be in future.
We are creatures capable

of compromise. The male's globular
organs, half-buried in his face,
are decorative stones. The woman's, holes.

Look for future crafts to explain flora. We've shot fauna
up, but brought them back. Understand
our sentimentality. Our nature
we call human. Other times, humane.

At the top of the plate, the hyperfine
transition of hydrogen. Two clefts
that bleed roughly twelve times
a year until they become stateless.

   All that we know

is expressed by the angle of the woman's
hip, cocked. The ball of her bare foot.

Please,

when you come, call us
Linda. And we will kiss
our own open palm and call you ours.

from *Arc Poetry Magazine*

The Play

A woman and I rest on the valley floor. The floor is smoothed with dead wood and varnish. In our hands we have space. We pull our hands apart and grow the space. It is a careful dance; there is much energy between two hands and the space is full of space that vibrates. I say space but say space that vibrates.[12]

A woman and I have come to meet and collide on the valley floor. This is beauty, this patience of two bodies with hands and their intimate cradling of space. Word is felt here. Here is the new and the known and the now and the hérna. All men and their sounds evaporate around us as we move our hands in unison.[13]

When a woman and I first enter the valley, we do not know one another. I am scared. There are sounds of men and their bright lights and none so tough as the wood and the snow. But there is so little wood anymore.[14]

At dawn, a woman wakes me and we run to the valley door and look outside and there we see the glacier. The glacier is sudden and terrible. Jökulhlaup.[15]

It is helpful to know some things and helpful not to know some things. It helps to know some things and then forget those things are known. For example, I know what to do if I am lost in an Icelandic forest. I know how to sit in a field and listen. But I forget the eruption. But I forget the flood. But I forget forget. Then, I feel isolated. At times, I feel isolated.[16]

Some things I tell no one.

A field is a room.[17]

12   In the middle of the day I travel. I travel. I travel.

13   I am in a day and my hands tremble.

14   I raise my arms, outstretched, to shoulder height and hold them there.

15   I hold my arms outstretched in front of me and will them to calm.

16   I inhale all I see and oxygen swarms through my arms, fidgeting energy through vein and bone. I inhale, stretch, push life to my fingertips. Block. Energy is the unknowable known, and words are clumsy as they form and tumble through the no-space space of my mind. I cannot tell if my hands tremble but my arms tremble as I hold them there—long, longer, lengthening—and I fill my lungs so full of breath my ribcage cracks. My arms crack. Each fine bone in my arm creaks and I exhale and lower my arms—tenderly, slowly, low—to rest quivering and warm by my sides.

17   Whinny and I'll be yours, I'll be yours, I'll gladly be yours.

from *Contemporary Verse 2*

BARDIA SINAEE ❧

Poem

Though they aren't found in the region
nightingales persist
in the poetry of the Americas

ringing in the end of the world
like Merwin's nightingale
in lofty oaks
in darkness

always darkness!

a bird that sings all day
a poet hears at night
and thinking nightingale
composes some didactic verse
that is more about himself
than what is probably
a robin

beware of what
what you say
says about you

in this way all poems are true
even the ugly ones

from *The Fiddlehead*

NATHAN MADER ☙

The Saturn and Sphinx Moths of the Upper Midwest

Let me speak of *The Saturn*
and Sphinx Moths of the Upper Midwest.

It's a map-sized Pocket Guide
laminated in a formaldehyde

of plastic that I've kept between my
Handbook to the Projectile Points

of Iowa and *The Selected Lyrics of Háfiz.*
Goes to show that we're all a bit

edited. Even *The Saturn and Sphinx*
Moths of the Upper Midwest is

cut to its completeness. The Vashti
sphinx moth flies to the light

bulb over our heads. The Death's
Head Hawk moth surfaces

in the *Silence of the Lambs*, alights
on the lips of Jodie Foster.

The Spiny Oakworm. The Honey
Locust. The Virginia Creeper.

That Gothic moth's an imposter.
The Polyphemus moth has four

eyes yet is named after the Cyclops
Odysseus blindsided by calling

himself "Nobody." A four-eyed
Cyclops moth is nobody, too.

Saturn moths are not a single species,
but moths swallowed by what

a system accrued. The "eyes" on
the wings of the Io moth are equal

to the widening inner aperture that
asks what kind of insect is prayer.

Close your eye, kid, and stare into Ovid.
Zeus transforms Io into a heifer

to hide her in plain sight. The cow
jumps into the moon like Li Po.

Anonymously carved into Wikipedia's
temple of light is the maxim: "there

are over 160,000 kinds of moths, many
of which are yet to be described."

The Abbot's sphinx. The Achemon.
Multimedia Lepidoptera. The Pink moth

denudes as it detaches from the synaptic
flash that cocoons it, ingesting

the muslin over its origins as Saturn
consumes the Sphinx. I once saw

an empty parking lot outside Fargo
deified by falling snow. I recall

the Upper Midwest as a system
of riddles and gods present

in the fluorescents of gas stations lit
like ashrams in which we might

dissolve our transverse orientation
to the things of this earth.

from *The Puritan*

SHANE BOOK ❧

S.T.A.R.S. (Strategic Tactical Armed Response Squad)

The forest clicked at me.
A lowered fence began
its creaking against the grass.
Mansions of corn, wind-flexed,
licked dudes sprawled
on the ground. Putative lemon de Ville
with the coupe leather seats,
cream soldiers, black berets
on big fro-ed heads. The force
is not something you want
to remember. It's the turtlenecks.
The dominating sugar
factory we lived in.
Pressed DOMINO's,
ready to light a river in two countries—
sorta enormous flotillas of checked
best Wyclefs, the brutal best friend,
a slap, a shot, slitting the pigs
and the thievery.
Pantherville,
let's see what settlements
we acquire. How many,
how many, how many   ,
how many. She know
she gotta
               keep me
some cash.
Until we're done
with all the thievery,
safeties off—
Next door homies gambling
on that game *Settlers of Wu Tang*.
Let's see what the settler does.

from *The Malahat Review*

MARGARET HOLLINGSWORTH ❧

Stone Faced

laurel
sings to stone
thanks tah roots
grabs limestone
thanks tah
limestone's crumbs
thanks tah amethyst
for rhododendron flower
glacier
dances rhododendron
into stone
sings fossil fah soh
slow
from stone we run
to stone
laurel leaf
encrypted

from *Contemporary Verse 2*

NANCY JO CULLEN ∞

TBH

1.

Teenagers are pulling their braces off with their bare hands
Illuminating the unlit valley of adolescence with their exposed midriffs
Subjecting mothers to the Sacrament of Contempt
Mothers are crying into their cold-pressed, non-gmo organic juice
The mothers of the mothers have had too much sun
Fragile little snowbirds, their bones are disintegrating
Such extremely low thresholds for enduring discomfort
They can't even; they just can't
Nobody asks to be born
Not to mention all that plastic accumulating in the landfill
When they said crisis response planning they meant anti-wrinkle cream
Accustom yourself to plaintive disregard
Nobody asks to be a YouTube instructional video gone wrong
Not to mention all that human trash accumulating in the belly of the whale

2.

Not to mention all that human trash accumulating in the belly of the whale
Nor the invisible doctrine of the invisible hand and its invisible backers
Nor the offshore holdings of the Father and the Son & Sons
Currently in a loss position for tax purposes
Devastating, that feeling we failed ourselves in the land of opportunity
The uncertain sickly appetite to please[1]
Think of something meaningful to say to the kids:
TBH, freedom for the pike is death for the minnows
The body keeps the score, our long history of anxiety
In the province of ongoing extirpation
Still, there is the miracle of the softening mud and dog shit, flagrant
Uproar of the Hermit Thrush, the White Throated Sparrow
The Brown Creeper, the Earth turning again toward warm days
The wonder of the Body, TBH, is its capacity for punishment

I   Sonnet 147

3.

The wonder of the body, TBH, is its capacity for punishment
We told our daughters, do not walk through that park; we said
You are a public space & it will not soon end
You are open for business 24/7, sweetheart
That age-old Madonna/"she has no respect for herself" divide
The need to think critically about a safe space
Say yes, say yes to the dress; say no
Say sorry, say my fault; say please
Anyway, what she can or can't eat is practically all she will think
About, a nuanced dance of tactics and selection
And the Instagram effect now that nature isn't natural
Confession of our faults is the next thing to innocence
Follow the thought of envy
The rich live, the rich live longer everywhere

4.

The rich live, the rich live longer everywhere
The rich think, the rich think about think-pieces
By think-piece they mean hip & knee replacement surgery
By hip and knee replacement surgery they mean inheritance
By inheritance they mean embrace sincerity
By embrace sincerity they mean deposit the proceeds of social conditioning
They mean to say, efficiency algorithms are their jam
They mean welcome to the so-called sharing economy
We push the walk button; we push the walk button again
We push the walk button again; we are on fire at the intersection
Our bones consumed in the noise, the weather
Some girls *imagine* they feel worse than they do
They get into a dither just by thinking too much about themselves[2]

5.

They get into a dither just by thinking too much about themselves
Their informational appliances are always at their fingertips
Their fingertips are always on the receiving end
Of the global supply chain, always on the receiving end
Of stand-out online dating profile photos

2   You're a Young Lady Now, 1961

Always on the receiving end of palatable versions of
Demographically segmented market variables
Always on the receiving end of the body in trouble
Brought on by an insufficiency of imagination & upcycled
Dresses; brought on by the absence of absence
And the plastic particulate matter of a bifurcated heart
Your continued participation serves as express consent
Bring your noise cancelling headphones
The Lord helps those who help themselves

6.

Because the Lord helps those who help themselves
Because all the cats want to dance with the natural mutation
Because of the heat trapping nature of sweet little sixteen
Because of the inability to recall the sequence of traumatic events
Because of the tendency of attention to be affected by recurring thoughts
Because of record breaking high temperatures
Because of mitigation and adaptation
Because of benzodiazepine
Because of twenty-one words used to describe only women
Because of sharks, dogs, mountains, elevators and mosquitoes
Because of black legged ticks and American presidential elections
Because of selective serotonin reuptake inhibitors
Because of smiley face emoticons
Because of clinical levels of acquisitiveness

7.

Because of clinical levels of acquisitiveness
And all the angels & saints in their "spiritual gangster" t-shirts
All the latest patrons of leisure, style, and taste
All the latest patrons of teenaged girls, angular and hungry
Feeling their supreme moment of destiny
Teenaged girls waiting to spring into time
And by time they mean take their husband's name
And by all the angels & saints they mean reality TV stars
They mean they have no sense of their over-determined circumstances
This poem is bitter; this poem has gone to fat

This poem is crushing the dreams of teenaged girls
It tells them they are still unloved
But those girls are laughing and this poem is an old bitch
And, teenagers are pulling their braces off with their bare hands

from *The Puritan*

DOYALI ISLAM ◌

– 31st parallel –

for the dead and the living

bird & fish world, gaza strip   1
  shrapnel   sears/
        steel crows

and mr. al-draimli's cats have ears
  soft as rose petals—and pink!

good for ages four & up
(esp. in cases of fear & fright)
  telephone 2860098
or visit downtown al-wahdah street

they mew. they eat. they some days
  look away from you with drawn
  faces, as men in wrinkled shirts
without cigarettes or much hope

    stones thrown are stars
      that lend no light,
    but mr. al-draimli's cats have
    eyes—glittering black moons

  nine times over, they will live
their lives in these cages, i think
      mr. al-draimli's cats

2   al-faraheen, gaza strip

after the disturbance, i gather
the small masses; fists forcing
    out new purpose
and cupping it like a baby bird

the machines raze bullishly but
what of diesel, debris and dust?
    i gather

wheatdust, water: i'll show you
i'll show you hope in a handful
      of dust

the way stars exploded offer up
new stars, my day's worth rises

my village queues and unshekels
herself, receives joyful; then

dry soil tautens to a foot drum
no night too aloof to witness

the processional of proud hands
each pair lifting ten suns

from *Arc Poetry Magazine*

JORDAN ABEL ❧

the tumbling water washes bones

A deep, narrow chasm. Black rocks. The river lies still on those black rocks.
A mile above there is a tumbling; there is a moment. At this very moment
there is a tumbling in the air a mile above us that runs straight through
the open heavens and into some other place. A deep hollow. No shape. No
consistency. No breaking some hundred feet in the air. Some places are softer
than others. Some hundred feet up in the air. Some right angles enter into
narrow passageways and some right angles break off a mile in the air above us.
These rocks are full of cracks. Water has worked through some deep hollows.
Breaking here. Wearing there. Breaking and wearing. Breaking and wearing
until the chasm separates into two caverns. Some hundred feet in the air there
is no danger. There is scattered driftwood and the scent of roses. There are
glimpses of roses and rocks and shrubs. There is a steep, rugged ascent. A path
that winds among the black rocks and trees. Somewhere in the air there is the
scent of roses. Somewhere out there is the wilderness. A reasonable distance
through scenes of greenery and nature and glimpses of mountain ranges that
disappear just as suddenly as they appear. Among the rocks and trees there are
mounds of earth and other rocks and other driftwood. Somewhere there is an
islet and another islet and a clear sheet of water and bald rocks just beneath
the surface. There are forests and straits and islets and rocks and somewhere
in the air is the scent of roses. There are crevices and fissures and rocks. The
rocks surround themselves in other rocks. Although there are sometimes
mounds of earth in between. On the shore, there are fragments of rocks. In
the deeper parts of the river, there is more tumbling. At this very moment,
the river pours into a wide fissure where it just becomes more water between
rocks. Between the broken rocks and the deep, roaring cavern there is the
scent of roses and driftwood and trees. There is light and straight, naked rocks
and immovable trees. There are woods and rivers. And the bed of that river
is ragged with rocks and intersecting ravines that cut silently across the water
above where somewhere in the air is the scent of roses. The woods are full
of sounds and rocks. The woods are full. The upper air, where it drifts over
the tops of trees, is full of sounds. Just where it breaks over the tops of trees
there are slow, intermingling drifts of sounds and scents that brush over the
clearing some fifty or sixty feet up in the air. Rocks and logs and mounds of
earth and narrow fissures and bottom land and little ponds and a brook that
shoots through the narrow fissures, spreading through moment after moment
of stretched light. There is a bellowing in the passageways between the rocks.
There are moments of admonished madness. There are moments spreading

over the acres of bottom land. There are precipices and adjacent lakes and head waters. There is a fierceness here that floats through the waters. These rivers are full to the brim. These waters stream down to our feet. In six hours these waters will rush in. And in another six hours these waters will rush out. Salt grows in this water. The water in the woods and on the great lakes and in the higher parts of the sea. Stretching out horizontally until the current flows upward like blood at the throat. On these waters the edges touch the shores and the deerpaths trace back to the streams. In the short distance in between the water and the black rocks is a deep shadow. The breath of the stream. The glancing waters. The throat of the river. These woods are full. Gliding above somewhere up in the impenetrable darkness is the scent of roses. Somewhere there is the sound of rushing waters ringing through the deep stillness of the night. The moon rises and the light glances here and there on the water and down to the river bed. At times, the light hangs in the air on the breath of the river. There are dark waters; there is night. This is the unmingled sweetness of air that sinks into the foaming waters. These are the vaults of forest. There is a stillness here somewhere in the wilderness. There is lightning and then there is stillness. There are echoes that rush through the forest until they disappear. A mile above there is a tumbling. In the foaming waters, there is the colour of blood gushed from some other place. Some other throat. Some other, softer place. Some waters carry the dead. Somewhere up in the air there is the scent of roses. Some flames last forever. Some waters thicken with limbs and bodies and trembling voices. Some waters are still. Somewhere in the velocity of the uproar there is a current of air. An unmingled sweetness that sinks in to the forest. The narrow path adjacent to the brook is full of bodies. The blood as natural as water. Glassy mirrors. The sunken hillsides. The shores. The black rocks between the mounds of earth. The glittering stars. The open air floating over the forest. In the valley, the stream overflows onto the banks. Here, the tumbling water washes bones and the waters of the river go in to the salt lake. There is a canopy from the woods spreading over the lake, shadowing a dark current with a deep hue. When the sun is setting, these waters become healing waters. But the sun is not setting and the current branches silently into the dark parts of the lake. Somewhere in the forest, bark is peeled from a tree. Branches break. For many minutes there is a struggle and a deep, cool wind. There is a current of air. There is silent motion plunging and glancing and sweeping over the broken branches. The sound from the rushing waters drifts through the air. There are words and yells and cries. As the air flows up from somewhere in the deep, narrow ravine, there is silence again. With the exception of the sounds that come from the rushing water.

from *The Capilano Review*

SHERYDA WARRENER ❦

Unpredictable Intervals

The Long Now Foundation's ongoing
art installation, a 10,000-year clock thrust

into the limestone cliffs of Snake Range
amidst bristlecone pines,

testament to our experimental temporal
rhythms. A peal set at unpredictable

intervals bewilders with each improvisational chime.
I press the button on the toaster that reads

A BIT MORE, send time out
the cat door to rewild, hold out

for the slice to leap up, a hearty indication
of novel measures. On the window sill,

the last of the fruit flies circle, a silk-winged
cloud. The funnel silvers

the flies down to the vinegar-sweet
trap I've laid, another pattern's demise.

A single ranunculus blooms, moon

to the planet of the table, reveals
its infinite dark side. Droplets

form at the foot of tights slung over
the showerstall to dry.

Even my molecular history
regenerates, imperceptible

to the naked eye. "Listen to water,"
admonishes the nearby waterline, and even

this pile-driver heart I've trained
myself to ignore begins its grind, though

by the time the rhythm reaches me, it's rendered
meaningless: I've fallen

behind. Off-centre, I'm still naïve enough

to believe I'm in this. Through the rectangle
portal of my kitchen I watch light

make of a face a sundial.
A crow goes off like a five-alarm fire.

Thousands of miles off, dwarf pines
lined along cliff-edge tick

in a wind that whips up,
distorts everything, then dies.

from *The Puritan*

FAITH ARKORFUL ☙

Vacation

And on the third day we went to Grand Etang and I
was still alive. Death digs its way into every vacation and in this
    homecoming
I grow larger, fall weaker. Canada, my body, a frozen lake.

This lake was poured into a volcano
stuck between dying and dead and
everyone has a different answer.

And for a brief moment I can see
what could be the entire history of me. My ancestors
bussin ah wine on the mountain peak and swimming
on the lakebed and grinding down with teeth like sugarcane splinters
the last bricks of the old church. Other strands, more mundane
are not allowed to come together
and fade without cure.

A black girl learns to worship herself very early. To not take invitations
from strangers. To tend to her own burns
and hide in the dark. After we return from Grand Etang
I realize I want to have it all.

I want to die and I want to do it
without my body having to give in to the water. Maybe all the love
I have for myself
just comes down to saying I have had a good run.
With throwing salt on all the ghosts, old and new
hands dipped in milk
trying to take a peek at your body
as if it was a thing that never belonged to you.

As if they could cut off the stem and
pretend it was never a plant
that called for sun and water and love beyond all interruptions

from *The Puritan*

KATHERENA VERMETTE ❦

when Louis Riel went crazy

1.

after the Red River "Rebellion" of 1869
Louis Riel went crazy, he ran off and hid
in a bush along the Seine, a land that jutted
out into the stream, a place
everyone called Vermette's Point, a thick
mass of thin trees, next to a narrow
slot of ploughed land and a meek
farmhouse, a brief place, nondescript
but the prideful home of my great-
great uncle and aunt
Riel stayed there a month, a long
month when spring
spread out slowly
separating him from his "crimes"
and my aunt left food at the bush's edge
for him, bannock lard and meat on an old tin plate
a meal for a dog, or
a "rebel,"
something he would have to hurry to
so the foxes didn't get there first
some say that's where Louis took
the name David, where in
his cold, hungry penitence
God spoke to him, gave him
his divine purpose
and a middle name
when Louis Riel was hanged in 1885
my great-great uncle had no land, Manitoba
had become a province, and Canadian
surveyors came in, Métis
homesteads were dissected,
bisected, halved, quartered
over and over again until
nothing was left, only

a square to balance one foot on
for only one second
before they all fell over
Ottawa took it all by then, all
those half-breed homesteads, ribbon lots not
"properly bought" were sold, and my
ancestral uncle's home was pulled
up from under him like a rug, a rug
rolled up from the river's edge all the way
to the road, tucked under
Canada's collective arm
and chucked on a eastbound train
with all the other rugs, all the other
rolled up land that became tidy
cylindrical tokens, conquered
presents to be presented
to John A., nothing more than
rolled-up grass like pressed cigars
he lit up and smoked
'til they were spent
only white
ash brushed off
red coats
and made
nothing

2.

there is still a place called Vermette, just
southeast of Winnipeg, landlocked but
not far from the river Seine, it has
a postal code, a store and a sign because
they let us use the names of our dead
as if that means
we're allowed to honour them
we do not forget our dead, we know
where they are, and sometimes we pull
them out of the ground like relics
we brush them off and wonder
at their possibility, like rotting bulbs of some

rare and fragile orchid, we tend to them
all winter and put them back
into the earth come spring with nothing
more tangible than hope to
make them flower
our names are scattered
seeds all over this
mother land, fathers' names
sons' names
Ritchot
Béliveau
Beaupré
just words long lost of meaning
Dumont
Desjarlais
Debuc
Leduc
south side street signs, markers
Tourenne
Turenne
Traverse
Trembley
this city is a graveyard
Guimond
Guiboche
Guibault
Gautier
my conquered people, these
children of bereft sons who
once thought themselves so grand
they had the nerve to create
a province
Carriere
Charriere
Chartrand
Cote
dead names breathing
thin dusty life
and Riel

Riel
everywhere Riel
we are intertwined within
this city, as if we belong
as if we are honoured

from *Taddle Creek*

CONTRIBUTORS' COMMENTARY AND BIOGRAPHIES ❧

JORDAN ABEL is a Nisga'a writer from BC. Currently, he is a PhD candidate at Simon Fraser University where his research concentrates on intergenerational trauma and Indigenous literature. He is the author of *The Place of Scraps* (winner of the Dorothy Livesay Poetry Prize), *Un/inhabited*, and *Injun* (winner of the Griffin Poetry Prize).

Of "the tumbling water washes bones," Abel writes, "this piece comes from a project that is conceptually derived from James Fenimore Cooper's novel *The Last of the Mohicans*. In the larger project (and in 'the tumbling water washes bones'), I weave together Cooper's descriptions of land (and terra nullius) with my own descriptions of land in order to dismantle Cooper's colonial text while also assembling a text that attends to Indigenous presence. I was originally inspired to begin this project after reading Roxanne Dunbar-Ortiz's book *An Indigenous Peoples' History of the United States*, where she makes the argument that Cooper's novel plays a role in reinventing the colonial origins of the United States, and in creating a narrative that was 'instrumental in nullifying guilt related to genocide.'"

FAITH ARKORFUL is a writer from Toronto. Her work has been published or is forthcoming in *Hobart, Canthius, Arc Poetry Magazine*, the *Puritan*, the *Hart House Review*, and more.

Arkorful writes, "'Vacation' is a poem focused on notions of belonging. What does it mean to call a place home? What does it mean to be a visitor? In 'Vacation,' I wanted to explore the question of what it means to belong to a place, and how the answer to that question for me is immutably tied to a colonial history rife with pain, violence, and exploitation."

BILLY-RAY BELCOURT is from the Driftpile Cree Nation. He is a PhD student in the Department of English & Film Studies at the University of Alberta. His debut collection of poems is *This Wound is a World* (Frontenac House, 2017), which won the 2018 Griffin Poetry Prize.

Belcourt writes, "'Love is a Moontime Teaching' began as a meditation on how love is handed down to us by moms and grandmas and sisters —moontime referring of course to Indigenous conceptions of womanhood. It then flowered into a bigger critique of all of that which stymies love and care in Indigenous social worlds and elsewhere. I wanted to paint a complex picture of scenes of suffering and trauma, one that wasn't mired in a perverse desire to see the wounded, but one that glimpsed the fragilities of being in a world we did not want. I also wanted to experiment with the rhetorical device called anadiplosis, which is when a poem uses a word near the end of the clause as the start of the next clause. This, to me, highlights the flexibility of language, how we can pit it against itself to expose meaning."

SELINA BOAN lives and works on the traditional, ancestral, unceded territories of the Musqueam, S̲k̲wx̲wú7mesh, and Tsleil-Waututh peoples. Her work has appeared in numerous literary journals including *Room*, *CV2* and the *New Quarterly*. She won the Gold National Magazine Award for Poetry in 2017 and was shortlisted for the 2016 CBC Poetry Prize. She is currently working on a collection of poems exploring her Cree and European heritage.

Of "inside the vein:," Boan writes, "This is a poem that threads together the personal and the political. That seeks to hold the possibility of memory, story, and embodied knowledge while also challenging the colonial construct of blood quantum, an assimilation tactic that also serves to delegitimize the sovereignty of Indigenous Nations. It is a poem that considers the ways the past, present, and future coexist. In the poem, I include the title of the installation 'rock paper river' by the visual artist Faye HeavyShield, whose work exploring identity, memory and place inspired the jumping off point for this poem. The first draft came tumbling out. I let my body take over; I followed the sounds. The quotes, by Monique Mojica and Bonita Lawrence, came later, along with the poem's shape. I felt it was important to draw in other voices, to provide additional context for the ideas I was circling inside the body of the poem. What stories do our bodies carry? What are my responsibilities as a person of settler and Cree heritage? At its core, 'inside the vein' is about identity, family, community, and belonging. It is a poem that considers how bodies can hold memory and the various forms inheritance can take."

SHANE BOOK lives in Ontario. His first collection, *Ceiling of Sticks*, won the Prairie Schooner Book Prize and the Great Lakes Colleges Association New Writers Award and was a Poetry Society of America "New Poet" Selection. His second volume, *Congotronic*, won the Archibald Lampman Award and was shortlisted for the Canadian Authors Association Award, Ottawa Book Award, and Griffin Poetry Prize. He is also a filmmaker whose award-winning work has screened around the world.

Of "S.T.A.R.S.," Book writes, "I don't like to explain my own work because I don't want to push one particular meaning. That just limits possibilities. And if poems do anything, they are sites of liberation, of what's possible. I want readers to have an experience in language, like diving into a pool made of words. So instead of talking about what it means, I'll highlight a few moments. First, the title. While writing the poem, I was reading about the history of Strategic Tactical Armed Response Teams like S.W.A.T. which employ tactics developed by U.S. forces in the Vietnam War. Basically, the idea was—and still is—for police to use military weapons and overwhelming force in civilian contexts; they are often used to subdue rebellious urban communities or in drug raids. The poem starts with pastoral images of a rural landscape, an ancient theme in literature. The references to black people sporting large Afros, wearing berets and turtlenecks, may remind a reader of iconic images of the Black Panther Party, founded as a community defence movement in 1966. Until it was removed in 2004, the Domino's sign lit the East River from the Brooklyn shoreline; a Domino's Sugar sign still lights the Baltimore harbour today. For centuries in the Americas, sugar, as a product, was harvested from the unpaid labour of enslaved Africans. The phrase 'Settlers of Wu Tang' echoes a board game called 'Settlers of Catan' where players try to colonize an island. OK, that's all I'll say."

TIM BOWLING is a native of the west coast and now lives in Edmonton. He has published a lucky thirteen collections of poetry as well as five novels and two works of nonfiction. His writing in each of these genres has received national prize recognition, and his entire body of work has been honoured with a fellowship from the Guggenheim Foundation.

Bowling writes, "Some poems almost write themselves, and this is one of them. When asked to contribute to *Refugium: Poems for the Pacific*, I thought about my childhood and youth in Ladner, BC, a town bordered by the Fraser River to the north and the Gulf of Georgia to the west. I had been a salmon fisherman out of Ladner to the age of thirty, so I've long had an intimate physical relationship with the creatures of the ocean and have often written about salmon, seals, killer whales, eagles. But what about the less visible and well-known coastal species? Well, they often have names that constitute mini-poems. And since poets adore lists, and since I like to employ humour in my writing, I decided to use the names of these other species to craft what is known as a found poem (a poem in which the poet basically puts down the words as he finds them). As for the insults, I guess that's a kind of found poem within a found poem, as I just took clichés of a certain type of macho confrontation and let loose. Overall, I was just doing what I've done since I was a kid: getting great joy out of putting words together. Poetry really is as simple as that. You don't believe me? Who do you think you are, the Lord dwarf-venus himself? Why, I oughta…"

DIONNE BRAND lives in Toronto. Her collections of poetry include *Ossuaries*, which won the Griffin Poetry Prize; *Land to Light On*, winner of the Governor General's Award for Poetry and the Trillium Book Award; *thirsty*, winner of the Pat Lowther Memorial Award; and *No Language is Neutral*. Brand was awarded the Harbourfront Festival Prize in 2006 and was Toronto's

Poet Laureate from 2009 to 2012. In 2017, she was appointed to the Order of Canada. Brand is a Professor of English in the School of English and Theatre Studies at the University of Guelph.

The "Versos" from *The Blue Clerk* appearing here are earlier versions of selections from the manuscript for Dionne Brand's collection, *The Blue Clerk: Ars Poetica in 59 Versos* (McClelland & Stewart, 2018.) The collection "stages a conversation and an argument between the poet and the Blue Clerk, who is the keeper of the poet's pages."

MIKE CHAULK lives on the Speed River in Guelph, Ontario, where he kisses his dog on the mouth and drives trucks full of beer for a living. His work has appeared in the *Malahat Review, PRISM, filling Station*, among other places. He has worked as a seaman in Labrador, Sweden, and Wales, and previously lived in Montreal for five years where he punched time as the associate poetry editor of *the Incongruous Quarterly* as well as the editor-in-chief of *the Void Magazine* at Concordia University.

Of "The Canada Goose," Chaulk writes, "This poem is part of a long series called *How Long Do Birds Live* that pits anxiety and indifference about the passage of time and opportunities against one another while wrestling with more or less mundane situations. I wrote this as I started more actively learning about my heritage, specifically the Labrador Inuit and Cree on my father's side. Though I grew up suburban in Guelph, Ontario, we visited Goose Bay often. Later, as an adult, I worked a few seasons as a deckhand on *The Northern Ranger*, a freight and passenger ferry that services the isolated communities on Labrador's North Coast. I learned a lot about people, the land, and hard work while I was over there; I made connections that are stronger than most ties I have in my life. I have long been trying to understand what heritage means to a person, how much weight it holds, and how this question butts up against the politics of claiming an identity. This is something I have struggled with a lot, so I set out to write a poem that would reflect my experience as a child negotiating my darker skin, of trips in Labrador learning family traditions, and of coming to accept my ability to claim that heritage in ways that I continue to interpret and negotiate. I don't know how to write about this properly, and that's a large part of what this poem is about."

GEORGE ELLIOTT CLARKE was born in Windsor, Nova Scotia, near the Black Loyalist community of Three Mile Plains, in 1960. He grew up in Halifax, Nova Scotia, as an Africadian—a member of the historical African-Nova Scotian community whose roots run three-centuries-deep in New Scotland. But his North American roots are still deeper, for Clarke is also Afro-Métis, a member of the Eastern Woodland Métis Nation Nova Scotia, and he doesn't give a damn if you don't like it! In fact, he sayeth, "To hell with you! If you can't accept the existence of Afro-Métis Canadians, just go ahead and die!" Clarke's work and life struggle against the Euro-Caucasian *erasure* of Canadians of Colour—a superficially pacific form of brutally violent white supremacy. Clarke's won a bunch of awards and is also an O.C., O.N.S., and F.R.C.G.S. Need the details? Look him up.

Of "Lincoln Plans for Peace (*Pace* Appomattox)," Clarke writes, "This poem is part of an epic poem, *Canticles I*, published in two volumes, *MMXVI* and *MMXVII* (Guernica Editions 2016 & 2017), treating the misery of white supremacist imperialism and the concomitant African Slave Trade, as well as resistance to these evils, from approximately Homer to Mao. The epic poem riffs off Ezra Pound's *Cantos* by staging a medley of dramatic monologues, many in the voices of historic(al) actors such as Abraham Lincoln or Cleopatra or Nanny-of-the-Maroons or St. Augustine or Nancy Cunard or Pound himself. Clarke believes that the only way to confront our mutual history of economic exploitation and racist/sexist oppression is to be asked to overhear the players themselves justifying their crimes or narrating their rebellions. In this case, we overhear Abe Lincoln reviewing the colossal slaughter of the U.S. Civil War, his ambivalence regarding black liberation, and expressing his hopes for a utopian future for himself and for the Republic."

DANI COUTURE lives in Toronto. She is the author of four collections of poetry and the novel *Algoma* (Invisible Publishing). Her work has been nominated for the Trillium Book Award for Poetry, given an honour of distinction from the Writers' Trust of Canada's Dayne Ogilvie Prize for Emerging LGBTQ writers and won the ReLit Award for Poetry. Her latest collection, *Listen Before Transmit*, was published by Wolsak & Wynn in 2018.

Of "Pioneer 14," Couture writes, "'Linda' is Linda Salzman Sagan. While Carl Sagan and Frank Drake designed the plaques for the Pioneer space probe, Salzman Sagan, an artist, prepared the artwork. As a condition of approval, NASA required the pudendal cleft be removed from the image of the woman. I wrote the poem after studying the plaque's design and reading the valid criticisms about it. In the end, the image of the figures included was not inclusive or fully representative of all humans on Earth and one of the figures that was included was edited so as to not appear 'pornographic.'"

NANCY JO CULLEN, a transplanted westerner, divides her time between Toronto and Kingston. She is the fourth recipient of the Writers' Trust Dayne Ogilvie Prize for LGBT Emerging Writers. Her poetry has been shortlisted for the Gerald Lampert Award, the Writers Guild of Alberta's Stephan G. Stephansson Award, the Alberta Publishers Trade Book Award and the W.O. Mitchell Calgary book prize. She is at work on her fourth collection of poems.

Of "TBH," Cullen writes, "In the spring of 2016 my daughter was feeling all the energy and excitement of finishing grade eleven and planning for her last fun summer before college. She was full of her own power and I loved seeing in her that vigour of adolescence. But I feared for her too, ever conscious of how unsafe this world is for girls and women. At the same time I was following the US nomination races. Donald Trump hadn't yet won but it seemed certain he would and my anxiety was kicking up a notch or ten. The resistance to Hillary Clinton was confounding to me; all that vitriol that is reserved especially for women. It seemed that the feminist work of the past 40-50 years had affected so little change, here in Canada as much as in the USA. I suppose I felt a little hopeless. Anything like the MeToo movement seemed impossible or, at least, decades away."

FAIZAL DEEN was born in Georgetown, Guyana. He immigrated to Canada in the late 1970s, settling in Ottawa where his father worked at the now defunct Canadian International Development Agency (CIDA). He studied English Literature and Language at Queen's University in Kingston, Ontario, before moving to Kingston, Jamaica in the early 1990s to teach at Jamaica College. His first poetry collection, *Land Without Chocolate, a Memoir* was published by Wolsak & Wynn in 1999, and remains Guyana's first LGB poetry collection. His second collection, *The Greatest Films*, was published by Mawenzi House in 2016 and marks a resumption of his poetry practice after a lengthy absence abroad. He remains a resident of Ottawa where he is working on an experimental novel, *The Arcade Master*, and a new poetry collection, *He Ancestral.*

Deen writes, "'Modern Politics' is exemplary of my insistence on formal and structural experimentation as an integral component of any Caribbean poetics of decolonization."

MICHAEL FRASER lives in Toronto. He has been published in numerous national and international anthologies and journals. He was published in *The Best Canadian Poetry in English 2013*. He won *Freefall's* 2014 and 2015 Poetry Contests. He won the 2016 CBC Poetry Prize. His latest book is *To Greet Yourself Arriving* (Tightrope Books, 2016).

On "African-Canadian in Union Blue," Fraser writes, "The poem is a first-person account of an African-Canadian soldier leaving the Union Army due to inadequate or non-existent pay, horrid living conditions, and animosity directed towards him from white Union soldiers and residents. The poem is from my current manuscript, which profiles and commemorates the lives of

African-Canadians (British North Americans at the time) who fought in the American Civil War. I'm fascinated that many of these individuals went to fight for the freedom of their African-American brethren while fully cognizant of the severe discrimination and outward enmity expressed by Union soldiers and residents. They were inadequately armed, underpaid, or not paid at all, poorly rationed, and suffered horribly in unsanitary training camps. Once engaged in battle, it was impossible for Black Union troops to surrender. Confederates did not recognize black soldiers as human. Thus, the conventions of surrender were never applied to black soldiers. This resulted in massacres of black troops, the most notorious being the Battle of the Crater, and Fort Pillow. White Union soldiers who surrendered were given quarter, shown mercy, while black troops were slaughtered."

SUE GOYETTE lives in Halifax and has published six books of poems and a novel. Her latest collection is *Penelope* (Gaspereau Press, 2017). Goyette teaches in the Creative Writing Program at Dalhousie University.

Goyette writes, "I wrote *Penelope* after re-reading the *Odyssey* and feeling a profound homesickness for her voice. I wondered at being stuck at home with a house full of suitors and a teenage son. And in my experience, waiting has kept me profoundly and actively alert and is its own species of epic so I thought she deserved her own poem. I had recently spent some time in hospital waiting rooms, in the close circle of caring for someone, which, in its way, felt epic. I was unmoored and didn't know how to pace myself because I didn't know what lay before us, I didn't know how long attending to this experience would take. This is true of all experiences, I guess. I wanted some company in this waiting (and in the fear that was tenacious and percolating) and Penelope's voice was the good company I craved. So I listened for her and here she is, wildly and actively engaged, waiting."

PHIL HALL lives in Ontario. His most recent books are *Guthrie Clothing: The Poetry of Phil Hall—a Selected Collage* (Sir Wilfrid Laurier University Press, 2015), *Conjugation* (BookThug, 2016), and—with Erin Mouré—*The Interrupted* (Beautiful Outlaw Press, 2017). He has won Canada's Governor General's Award for Poetry in English (2011), and also Ontario's Trillium Award (2012). He has twice been nominated for the Griffin Poetry Prize. He is the director of The Page Lectures at Queen's University.

Of "The Lyric," Hall writes, "In my lifetime metaphor has had one master: Tomas Tranströmer. When he died, I had the two dreams that are in this poem. And I once heard a fiddle made in prison out of matchsticks. The lyric cannot be corporate or choral, but only a solo against the odds."

MARGARET HOLLINGSWORTH lives in Toronto. Her poems have been published in literary magazines across Canada. She is best known as an award-winning dramatist and has also published a novel, *Be Quiet*, and a collection of short stories, *Smiling under Water*. One of her stories, "Tulips," appears in *Best Canadian Stories*.

Hollingsworth writes, "Like music, 'Stone Faced' comes to life when it is listened to. The notes of the scale are unchanging and the insistent rhythm of the poem is designed to reflect the speed of the repeating cycle of rebirth, growth, and death in nature. The fossil is memory cast in stone. The cycle continues."

LIZ HOWARD was born and raised on Treaty 9 territory in northern Ontario. Her book *Infinite Citizen of the Shaking Tent* won the 2016 Griffin Poetry Prize, the first time the prize has been awarded to a debut collection. Her recent work has appeared in *Poetry*, *Camera Austria*, and the *Walrus*. She is of mixed European and Anishinaabe descent, and is currently the 2018-2019 Canadian Writer-in-Residence at the University of Calgary.

Of "As if Our Future Past Bore a Bad Algorithm," Howard writes, "Can we agree that there is a lot going on in this poem? Both the title and the poem's opening line, 'A few particles ambushed the past,' seem to suggest that we find ourselves perhaps in a physics laboratory, if but a complicated one, romantically. But then the poem shifts quickly through several images/references: a televised laugh track, a scalp, gold, and a credit system. Where have we arrived and where are we going? These are the essential questions of the poem as well as can we ever be so sure of our own account of the past, our memory? The poem is slippery, fast, moving via "jump cuts," a technique borrowed from cinema, where we are rapidly shifting from scene to scene. The poem's central sequence contains a direct account of my personal family history. A kind of anchor. Then the tail of the poem-comet spins out again. With its spray of language and references. There is the appearance of the mind-brain that is the supreme conductor of all experience. Then also the levelling of direct experience with the witnessing of a stranger relieving himself in front of me. In the poem somehow I tie that to reading earlier in the day about an archaeological find of an ancient boy in the roots of a tree. As if our future past. I want to show how poetry can hold all of this."

AISHA SASHA JOHN was born in Montreal and lives in Toronto. She is the author of three poetry collections: *The Shining Material* (Book*hug, 2011), *THOU* (Book*hug, 2014), and the 2018 Griffin Poetry Prize shortlisted *I have to live* (McClelland & Stewart, 2017).

Of "CONDITIONS OF ENGAGEMENT," John writes, "I feel safe and free and I have direction in form. Double-spacing a poem and writing in all caps for me creates a simple and clear structure to name the objects of my consciousness. I like making and reading poems that reveal how a mind actually moves."

DOYALI ISLAM lives in Toronto. Her second poetry book is *heft* (McClelland & Stewart, 2019). Poems from this collection can be found in *Kenyon Review Online, the Fiddlehead,* and CBC Radio's *The Sunday Edition.* An award-winning poet and 2017 National Magazine Award finalist, Islam is the inventor of two poetic forms: the *parallel poem* and the *split sonnet.* She is poetry editor of *Arc Poetry Magazine,* and she exudes an undying love of cats—especially seniors. doyalifarahislam.com

Islam writes, "In 2010, I invented a new poetic form, which I coined the *parallel poem,* and of which ' – 31st parallel – ' is one example. (The form works with latitude lines [parallels]. A typical *parallel poem* grounds its halves [sub-poems] in distinct geographic locations/spaces, and works within a particular self-imposed constraint: count the characters, including spaces, in the various lines of ' – 31st parallel – .' Many contain 31.) In 2013, when writing this poem, I was married and living in North Bay, ON. My husband's tabby, Poncho, brought me comfort and joy, and I wondered: what value did pets have for children who were living under oppressive conditions? My cat-nature led me to a 2009 *Time* article, 'Raising Cats in Gaza: A Pet-store Owner's Lament.' The first half of ' – 31st parallel – ' felt dead until the cats crept in and became a metaphor for Gazans. And what can I say of the second half? I was curious about community bread-ovens—more common in the so-called Middle East—and came across a 2009 article, 'No Small Enterprise: Al-Faraheen's Community Bread Oven.' It relayed how a village local, Mohammed Abu Dagga, had drawn on long-held regional knowledge to build a diesel-operated mud-and-straw oven. Diesel was plentiful; cooking gas was scarce. ' – 31st parallel – ' exists because I was moved by human resilience and resourcefulness—the ability to use ingeniously the materials at one's disposal for personal and community survival. ...What kind of language offers that?"

SONNET L'ABBÉ lives and writes in Nanaimo, on the traditional territory of the Snuneymuxw. Her most recent publication is *Anima Canadensis,* which won the 2016 bpNichol Chapbook prize. Her forthcoming collection is *Sonnet's Shakespeare* (McClelland & Stewart, 2019), in which she overwrites all 154 of Shakespeare's sonnets.

L'Abbé writes, "'CII' is the 102nd poem of a book project called *Sonnet's Shakespeare,* in which I 'write over' all 154 of Shakespeare's sonnets. Within each prose-poem block, the original Shakespearean poem sits. I have displaced and surrounded Shakespeare's letters with my own, such that the original poem is rendered barely visible, audible only in moments and fragments. I wanted to create a form that spoke to a dynamic of cultural erasure, to show how English sits in relation to my racialized experience, and to grapple with the culture that has surrounded me to the point that it speaks through me. The first lines of Sonnet 102 are 'My love is strengthen'd, though more weak in seeming; / I love not less, though less the show appear'—you will perhaps be able to see how this language persists in my erasure. I hope the poem speaks for itself as far as how it sees an unrequited work crush happening in the wake of the Transatlantic slave trade."

TESS LIEM's debut full-length collection of poetry is *Obits* (Coach House, 2018). Her chapbook, *Tell everybody I say hi*, is available from Anstruther. Her writings appear on *Plenitude*, the *Puritan*, the *Town Crier*, *carte blanche*, and in *Room Magazine*, the *Walrus*, *Vallum* and elsewhere. "Rice Cracker" was the winner of the 2015 Constance Rooke Creative Nonfiction prize from the *Malahat Review*. She lives in Montreal, Tio'tia:ke, the traditional territory of the Kanien'kehá:ka Nation.

Liem writes, "'Anonymous Woman Elegy,' along with many of the poems in my collection, *Obits*, is indebted to an essay by France Théoret called 'Elegy for the Memory of Women.' Théoret writes in elegant circles describing the necessity of memory and memoir for both an individual and a group."

CANISIA LUBRIN, writer, educator and editor, was born in St. Lucia and now lives in Whitby, Ontario. Her reviews, poems, short fiction and nonfiction have appeared in journals and anthologies such as *the Unpublished City*, *Brick*, *Vallum*, and *the Rusty Toque*. Lubrin's debut poetry collection *Voodoo Hypothesis* (Wolsak & Wynn, 2017), finalist for the Gerald Lampert Award, Pat Lowther Award, and Raymond Souster Award, has garnered honours, including being named a CBC Best Poetry Book of 2017.

Of "Final Prayer in the Cathedral of the Immaculate Conception II," Lubrin writes, "Here's an attempt to characterize something inimical to the act of letting go—sometimes the only sane thing to do. The poem, in nonlinear time like a pinball, asks for brief illuminations to its questions before quickly moving on to unknown dispersals of its family tree before it must, inevitably, end. But there is nothing to hold its lines too long in place. No guarantor to afford it a cleanly locatable thesis about what it means to have faith or to belong. An irony is the greater teacher: this intimation of abandonment can in some ways scaffold one's sense of truer belonging. The stuff of what determines a belief in belonging extends to speech. And since language is inherent to the project of poetry, whose very anatomy is music, the song and celebration premised in the mode of its creation is troubled in that questioning of a faith in words—as prayer. Offered here are the polyvocal rhythms of tracing the creolized landscapes that riddle the islands of the Caribbean over our long colonial history. Offered, too, is a diaspora peopled through the very act of mining the complexly unique, simultaneously exilic and concentric circumstances of diaspora. People charged by their own insistence to be alive and to be. But without a safe place to disembark, without a place to claim and to be tethered to, here is, eventually, to reckon a re-entering into humanity, into speech, into body, into life beyond the trauma of unbelonging. The black body, then, is undeniably always the modern self."

ELI TAREQ LYNCH is a poet working in Montreal. They have work in *THEM*, the *Puritan*, *carte blanche*, the *Shade Journal*, the *New Quarterly*, and elsewhere. They were one of the organizers of the Off the Page 2016 literary festival and participated in the Banff Centre's "Centering Ourselves" residency.

Of "After Samiya Bashir's Field Theories," Lynch writes, "This poem comes out of frustration but also affection. I've been part of different BIPOC writing communities in Montreal (Tio'tia:ke) and Canada that have really nurtured me and my writing practise, but that also weren't this utopic ideal that I think sometimes people imagine happens when BIPOC get together. It's a lot more complicated and there's a lot of lateral violence, tensions, and racism that happens between BIPOC that is hard to address when trying to first deal with the overwhelming oppression of white supremacy. This poem tries to complicate the idea of the utopic BIPOC space but also tries to relay the positive experiences I've had sharing space with other marginalized writers. There was a particular tense conversation that happened in my friend Cason's living room, which is where this poem began. I then decided to layer in other moments from history and pop culture that address these intersections of identity. Recently I've decided to mostly write for and to other queer writers and writers of colour and it's really changed the way I write and read for the better."

NATHAN MADER was born in Regina, Saskatchewan and currently lives in Kyoto, Japan. He received his M.A. in Creative Writing and English from the University of Regina after working as a commercial roofer for a number of years in Victoria, BC. Recent poems have appeared in *Vallum*, *Prism*, the *Fiddlehead*, *Grain*, and the *Puritan*, and he has been a finalist for the *Walrus* Poetry Prize.

Of "The Saturn and Sphinx Moths of the Upper Midwest," Mader writes, "The poem comes from a pamphlet I purchased at a nature preserve just outside of Coralville, Iowa, that reappeared when I pulled my favorite version of the great Persian poet Háfiz off the shelf. My mind half attuned to the spirit of Háfiz, I found the names of the moths became charged with a larger-than-life energy—'The Spiny Oakworm. The Honey/ Locust. The Virginia Creeper'—that began to call forth something new. As the poem emerged, I started to see how the way moths know where they are by a 'transverse orientation' to light while being hopelessly drawn to it was similar to the way the language surrounding the moths attracted me. The guest-appearances of Homer's cyclops and Odysseus (as 'Nobody'), the echoes of Emily Dickinson ('I'm Nobody! Who Are You?'), and the nod to Li Po's death (who, according to legend, drowned by trying to embrace the reflection of the moon) suggest that poetry, specifically metaphor, is also created by a kind of 'transverse orientation' to the light of language. Ultimately, the poem seems to believe that whatever it is in us, whether we write poems or not, that can make such real or imagined connections is also behind a relationship to the spiritual realm—that a single 'gas station' somewhere in the Midwestern darkness can light up a part of ourselves that offers a flightpath outside of the material world while giving us a sense of our place in it."

DAPHNE MARLATT lives in Vancouver. She's a poet and novelist known for her cross-genre work, particularly her poem cycle *Steveston* with photographs by Robert Minden. Recent titles are *Liquidities: Vancouver Poems Then and Now* (2013) and *Reading Sveva* (2016), a poetic response to the work of Italian Canadian artist Sveva Caetani. In 2017 Talonbooks published her *Intertidal: Collected Earlier Poems 1968-2008*, edited by Susan Holbrook. Marlatt was awarded the 2012 George Woodcock Lifetime Achievement Award.

Marlatt writes, "Having lived in Penang, Malaysia during my childhood and not having revisited since the mid-1980s, I was excited to 'go back,' but what was 'then' still resonates in what is 'now.' Particularly in George Town because it is protected and being restored as a UNESCO World Heritage Site so there are many British colonial buildings still standing in the vital multicultural, multi-religious, and multiracial energies of its streets today. Walking those streets I experienced astonishing jolts of memory mixed with perceptions of how things had changed. Then, to come home to the relatively new city of Vancouver was a further jolt. This poem was the first I tried to write in jet-lagged early morning, neither 'here' nor 'there,' no longer 'then' but not quite 'now' in the link between tropical George Town's sudden dusk and northern Vancouver's half-lit early morning, 'l'heure bleue.'"

MARGARET MCLEOD lives in Fredericton, New Brunswick with her husband and daughter. Her work has appeared in the *Amethyst Review*, the *Antigonish Review*, *Contemporary Verse 2*, the *Cormorant*, the *Dalhousie Review*,

Event, Fiddlehead, the *Nashwaak Review, Nod,* the *Potomac Review, Pottersfield Portfolio* and *Room*. She is currently working on a poem cycle, tentatively titled "Women of War." The first of these, "Helen of War," will be appearing in the new anthology *Making Monsters,* from Futurefire Publishing.

McLeod writes, "It's a ghost story, and everybody loves a good ghost story. Long ago, I rented an apartment for a while because it was supposed to be haunted. I never saw a ghost there, but something struck me, just out of the black—the single word, 'boneknockers.' So I wrote some drafts and put them away for a few weeks to marinate. Stuff happened. I moved. Weeks turned into years, and then decades. One day in 2016, an old diskette surfaced, with those drafts on them. I don't believe in ghosts anymore, but I do love a good ghost story. And here it is—twenty years in the making."

DANIEL DAVID MOSES lives in Kingston, Ontario, where he writes plays, poems and essays. The plays include *Coyote City, The Indian Medicine Shows,* and *Almighty Voice and His Wife,* the Canadian play in the Norton Anthology of Drama. His poetry collections include *Sixteen Jesuses, River Range Poems* (a CD) and *'A Small Essay on the Largeness of Light' and Other Poems.* His essays are collected in *Pursued by a Bear: Talks, Monologues and Tales.* In 2015 he received the OAC Aboriginal Arts Award.

"Once upon a time, in the fall of 2002," writes Moses, "Jim Millan, at the time artistic director of Crow's Theatre, did a production of an English language translation of the play 'Godzilla', by Yasuhiko Ohashi. The play, a parody of manners about changing social conventions in postwar Japan as illustrated by the courtship of the saurian monster and a human girl, charmed me. The following August, I went to Japan with singer ElizaBeth Hill and painter Shelley Niro to attend the Hiroshima Ceremonies and look for the Ainu, Japan's indigenous people. On our last day, in Tokyo, after souvenir shopping, we also found performances of Kabuki theatre and agreed that the aesthetic reminded us of powwow. When I heard the story of the Dene miners who also journeyed to Japan, looking for forgiveness for their part in that inhuman moment (they dug up the pitchblende used in those first atomic bombs), I knew I had to find a ceremony to put it all together."

SACHIKO MURAKAMI teaches, edits, and writes in Toronto, on territory included in the Dish With One Spoon Wampum Belt Covenant, and which is the traditional territory of the Anishinabek (most recently the Mississaugas of the New Credit), the Haudenosaunee Confederacy, and the Huron-Wendat. She is the author of three collections of poetry: *The Invisibility Exhibit* (Talonbooks 2008), *Rebuild* (Talonbooks 2011), and *Get Me Out of*

Here (Talonbooks 2015). She has been a literary worker for numerous presses, journals, and organizations.

Of "Good God/Bad God," Murakami writes, "This poem comes from my manuscript-in-progress, *Render*, which concerns itself with dreams, trauma, and recovery. This poem's form was inspired by dream dictionaries, which claim to explain the meanings of objects and visions in dreams. For example, in *10,000 Dreams Interpreted* (Coles, 1980), the entry for lentil enlightens the dreamer thusly: 'If you dream of *lentils*, it denotes quarrels and unhealthy surroundings. For a young woman, this dream portends dissatisfaction with her lover, but parental advice will cause her to accept the inevitable.' 'Good God/Bad God' takes this form and turns it on its head, in that its abstract headings perform the interpretive work on the material of each entry. The content of the entries come from my dream journal; I had noticed that I regularly dream about dogs. I have more or less always had a dog following me here and there, in waking life and in my dreams. My relationship with the divine, on the other hand, has been more problematic."

ERIN NOTEBOOM was born in Iowa and raised in Nebraska, but now writes out of a garden shed in Kitchener, Ontario. Her poetry has won the CBC Literary Award and been shortlisted for the Pat Lowther Award and the National Magazine Award. She is the author of two collections, both from Wolsak & Wynn. She also has five novels and a secret identity as Erin Bow, one of Canada's best writers for children.

Noteboom writes, "I used to be a physicist, and now I'm a writer. Everyone tells me that's a big leap, but I have found it remarkably small, which is perhaps why I am working on a collection of poems about science and scientists. 'Pavlovsk Station' is from that collection. It's a true story, but only part of one. Pavlovsk Experimental Station, on the outskirts of St. Petersburg, was founded in 1927 as the very first of the seed banks: caches of genetic diversity that humankind can fall back on after a disaster. Rare wheat varieties saved at Pavlovsk Station helped Ethiopia recover after a drought; different seeds replanted the Balkans after a war. During WWII, the station itself was overrun, but the scientists managed to dig up their tubers and rescue their seeds. They locked these and themselves away in secret vaults, and there, one by one, they starved to death. Twelve of them died, but none of them ate the seeds they were protecting. Science is not a body of knowledge, but a lens through which to view the world. Those who spend their lives with that lens may come to view the world differently. It may ask different things of them. Yet they remain—my poems would like to insist—poets, and human."

ARLEEN PARÉ grew up in Montreal, lived for three decades in Vancouver, and now lives and writes in Victoria. Her writing has appeared in a number of Canadian literary journals including the *Malahat Review, CVII, Eighteen Bridges*, the *Maynard*, the *Literary Review of Canada*, and *Geist*. She has five collections of poetry, two of which are cross-genre. She has been short-listed for the Dorothy Livesay BC Award for Poetry, and has won a Victoria Butler Book Prize, a CBC Bookie Award, and a Governor Generals' Award for Poetry.

Of "Come the Ungulate," Paré writes, "What I most enjoy about writing poetry is finding the right form for the poem and its subject. When I first heard Stephen Collis read his brilliant poem, 'Come the Revolution,' I enjoyed it for its radical message, but I most especially enjoyed it for the form he used. I have been writing a collection of poems about city streets called Earle Street, which will be released in 2020. And so, when I thought about the deer population in Victoria, which causes Victoria's citizenry a great deal of consternation, I rather shamelessly decided to borrow Stephen's form. True, the ever-present, irrepressible presence of deer in urban settings on Vancouver Island is a less serious subject, but I could not resist. I thank Stephen from the bottom of my thieving heart."

JOHN PASS lives on BC's Sunshine Coast. His poems have appeared in nineteen books and chapbooks in Canada, and in magazines in the US, the UK, Ireland and the Czech Republic. He won the Governor General's Award for Poetry in 2006 for *Stumbling in the Bloom* and the Dorothy Livesay Poetry Prize (BC Book Award) in 2012 for *crawlspace*. His most recent book is *Forecast: Selected Early Poems 1970–1990* (Harbour 2015). "Deer" is included in *This Was the River*, forthcoming from Harbour.

Pass writes, "'Deer' is one of a sequence of poems, *Creation of the Animals*, intrigued by what we make of animals, and by what they might create in us. In 'Deer', poetry and inhabiting a piece of land (and maybe lucking into dinner) are our directives; an uneasy, enveloping alertness is theirs. Waiting, watching, we can share. Also step, and browse. Ponder, so far as we know, is ours alone. The poem takes a swerve into our culture's most strikingly dramatic common instance of human/deer encounter, a deer struck on the highway. (Memorable poems on the subject abound: 'Travelling through the Dark' by William Stafford, 'Deer Hit' by Jon Loomis, and, if we substitute a moose, 'That Night We Were Ravenous' by John Steffler, to name a few.) But the struck deer here disappears. Survives? And the poem's through-line, its destination, is asking 'the first question'; formal but hungry, timelessly attentive, 'it listens' where a world valued by both species (of vegetable gardens, fruit trees, roses!) abides. Of course I believe there's more to the poem than this brief exegesis. The role of water, for example. Or the realtor. The gender roles. The soft vowels. All these and more, I leave to you, reader, to ponder."

PEARL PIRIE thrives in the wilds of Quebec, on rock, over lake and swamp. She has published three collections, and almost two dozen chapbooks. Her latest chapbook is *Sex in Sevens* (above/ground press, 2016). Her latest book is *the pet radish, shrunken* (Book*hug, 2015) which won the Archibald Lampman Poetry Award. A former director of the Tree Reading Series, and president of the KaDo haiku and tanka group, she has a couple manuscripts circulating. www.pearlpirie.com

Of "Misremembering the Colour of Books, A Something Something in Canada Where," Pirie writes, "The title came from an absent-minded self-deprecating comment I made on twitter after live-tweeting looking for a certain book, not being able to remember the title or author, only the contents and colour. Turned out that the cover-colour was different from the spine-colour. I tweeted, 'Misremembering the colour of books, a something something' to which Billy Mavreas said that sounds like a Pearl Poem Title. So I put it in the file of titles looking for poems, and of lines and of words looking for poems to congeal with. A couple people advised my denser poems needed more airspace in them to pace the digestion. The eventual result is a country-tweak for the surreal manuscript (est. completion, 2080) coloured by the new context of life: rural pace, cattle and swayback barns."

SHARRON PROULX-TURNER was a member of the Métis Nation of Alberta. Originally from the Ottawa River Valley, Sharron was from Mohawk, Wyandat, Algonquin, Ojibwe, Mi'kmaw, French and Irish ancestry. Sharron was a two-spirit nokomis, mom, writer and community worker. *Where the Rivers Join* (Beckylane, 1995), a memoir, was a finalist for the Edna Staebler Award for creative non-fiction, and *what the auntys say* (2002), was a finalist for the Gerald Lampert Award. Proulx-Turner died in 2016.

"the longhouse" appears in the late Sharron Proulx-Turner's last book, *creole métisse of french canada, me* (Kegedonce Press, 2017). According to editor Aruna Srivastava, as quoted in an interview with All Lit Up Canada, the collection "explores two-spiritedness and Métis history and questions of identity, and is focused as well on family history. The metaphor and reality of house(s) and home(s) are the thru-line of the book."

MEREDITH QUARTERMAIN was born in Toronto, grew up in the Kootenays, and now lives in Vancouver. She is the author of seven books of poetry and fiction, most recently *U Girl*. Her first collection of poems, *Vancouver Walking,* won the Dorothy Livesay Poetry Prize in 2006. Working with other writers during her time as Writer-in-Residence at Vancouver Public Library, and as Poetry Mentor at the SFU Writer's Studio, has been especially important to her.

Of "Letter to bp on Train Crossing the Rockies," Quartermain writes, "In 2015 and 2016 I travelled from the west to the east coast by train, keeping a notebook on the trip. I later discovered that Canadian poet bp Nichol (1944-1988) had made the same journey and recorded his reflections on it in Book VI of his *Martyrology*. As I wrote poems about my trip, I got into conversation with Nichol and his poems. Sometimes I called him 'Horseman' because of his famous group of sound poets The Four Horsemen. 'Letter to bp …' begins with a phrase from Nichol's poem and then includes things I saw from the train window such as the signs for Moose Lake and Swan Landing and the CN signs, as well as some of the train announcements which are in French and English. The bartender is a key figure on cross-Canada trains, entertaining dome-car passengers with facts about the surrounding country. So I included some of the facts I heard about Alberta, and some of the matter-of-fact signage I saw from the window. But somehow all these facts were irrelevant to the deep history of the land I could see. What did they have to do with the forces that had made the mountains? How could a few puny names imposed by recent settlers really connect me to this land and to the real nature of nationhood? Taking the guise of Odyssea, I set out to explore these questions."

SHAZIA HAFIZ RAMJI makes a home in Vancouver. Her first book of poems, *Port of Being* (Invisible Publishing, 2018), won the Robert Kroetsch Award for Innovative Poetry. She also wrote a chapbook, *Prosopopoeia* (Anstruther Press, 2017), and was a finalist for the National Magazine Awards and the Alberta Magazine Awards. Her fiction is forthcoming in the *Humber Literary Review*, and her essays and criticism have appeared in *Quill & Quire*, *Hamilton Review of Books*, *subTerrain*, and *Canadian Literature*.

Ramji writes, "'Astronaut Family' arose from the language of the housing crisis in Vancouver. The phrase has its origins in transnational migration and refers to families whose members live in different parts of the world in order to earn money (through investment in housing, made possible by the exploitation of tax and residency loopholes). Though I didn't know any investors, I was painfully aware of the ideology of flexible citizenship and how it changed the structure of my own relationships; many of my friends moved to other cities because they could no longer afford to pay rent in Vancouver, where I often wondered if I could write and live at the same time. Words like 'growth,' 'development,' and 'community' are consistently used in marketing, alienating people from local values and ethics—but the people who write these ads are people like me: cultural workers who are implicated and involved in creating the very thing they are trying to work against in order to live. In writing

'Astronaut Family,' I wanted to explore this double bind to take language back and make it mean, to imbue this historical moment with what I hope is compassionate resistance, the sort that binds people across distances."

a rawlings lives in Iceland. Her books include *Wide slumber for lepidopterists* (Coach House Books, 2006), *o w n* (CUE BOOKS, 2015), and *si tu* (MaMa, 2017). Her libretti include *Bodiless* (for Gabrielle Herbst, 2014) and *Longitude* (for Davíð Brynjar Franzson, 2014). rawlings is half the new-music duo Moss Moss Not Moss (with Rebecca Bruton) and the polypoetry duo Völva (with Maja Jantar). Her play *Áfall/Trauma* was shortlisted for the 2013 Leslie Scalapino Award. arawlings.is

rawlings writes, "While undergoing breast cancer treatment, I wrote the manuscript *Áfall/Trauma* as a series of scripts that capture *lived* performance. Icelandic language acquisition, cancer experience, and ritual exploration of the Icelandic countryside suture themselves into each script of *Áfall/Trauma* as a way to confront situational dysfluency. Included here is one script, entitled 'The Play.' This script documents, in part, earlier experiences I'd had with contact improvisation while in Toronto at the world's longest-running contact improv jam, co-organized by John Oswald and Pam Johnson. I transplanted these intimate improvisations within Iceland, the country where I live and where I underwent cancer treatment."

ROBIN RICHARDSON lives in Toronto. She is the author of three collections of poetry, and is editor-in-chief at *Minola Review*. Her work has appeared in *Salon, Poetry*, the *Walrus, Hazlitt*, and *Tin House*, among others. She holds an MFA in Writing from Sarah Lawrence College, has won the Fortnight Poetry Prize in the U.K., the John B. Santorini Award, the Joan T. Baldwin Award, and has been shortlisted for the CBC, *Walrus*, and *Arc* poetry prizes, among others. Richardson's latest collection, *Sit How You Want*, is out now with Véhicule Press. www.sithowyouwant.org

Of "Disembodied at the Botanical Gardens," Richardson writes, "This poem is a prayer. It owes a lot to Saint Francis."

YUSUF SAADI lives in Mississauga, Ontario. His writing has appeared in journals including *Hamilton Arts & Letters, Vallum, Brick*, the *Malahat Review, PRISM*, and *CV2*. His debut chapbook won the 2016 *Vallum* chapbook award. He holds a BA from York University and an MA from the University of Victoria.

Of "Belittle," Saadi writes, "I wrote this poem for someone once close to me who was traumatized by her abusive childhood. I think the poem is about different kinds of intimacy being held and lost, including the kind between the narrator and the woman it's addressed to—how words can be vehicles for intimacy, and how that intimacy lingers, however weakly, in language, even when it may have dissipated between the people themselves. The poem revolves around childhood violence, which is another kind of intimacy, but through a dark mirror. While a word has connotative and denotative meanings, it may also have personal associations like an aura around it, preventing us from reaching the word's neutral meaning, even if we want to escape into it. For me, the memories attached to the words in the poem are bittersweet; there's a minor gratitude in remembering the person I was close to, but also an awareness that she continues to face the trauma that I rarely need to think about. I wrote this poem when I was younger, and it was the first time I'd really thought about how certain words orbit around people, and people certain words."

BREN SIMMERS lives in Sackville, NB. She is the author of two books of poetry, *Night Gears* (2010) and *Hastings-Sunrise* (2015), which was a finalist for the City of Vancouver Book Award. Recent work has been published in *Refugium: Poems for the Pacific* and in the *Malahat Review, Event, Arc, CV2* and *Room*. She is working on a third poetry manuscript that explores changing community identity and resilience in Howe Sound, BC, over the last 100 years.

Of "If Spring," Simmers writes, "No matter where I am living, spring can't come soon enough. I wrote this poem a few years ago while on Galiano Island in February. The weather was mild, and in the woods, amidst the cedars, the salmonberries were just starting to blossom. Watching flocks of kinglets passing through the treetops, hearing their tinny bells, brought me a sense of hope and sparked the idea of living in the conditional. I wanted to capture that feeling of waiting for change, of waking up. That feeling of pushing beyond your boundaries in times of transition. What I particularly love about springtime is the experience of becoming fully alive again. Reflecting the explosion of new growth in that season, the anaphora form creates an incantatory rhythm that generates energy as it unfolds. Even through a repetitive cycle, change and transformation are possible."

BARDIA SINAEE was born in Tehran, Iran, and lives in Toronto. His poems have appeared in magazines across Canada and in previous editions of *Best Canadian Poetry in English*. He is the author of the chapbooks *Blue Night Express* (Anstruther Press, 2015) and *Salamander Festival* (Odourless Press, 2018). He is an MFA student at Guelph-Humber.

Of "Poem," Sinaee writes, "At the very back of my apartment is a tiny sunroom. This room contains my desk and a number of plants: an elephant palm, a rubber fig, a jade, a money tree, a zebra cactus, and a geranium that has never bloomed. The windows overlook a shared back yard. Sometimes when I'm at my desk in the afternoon, the neighbour steps out to hang laundry or dote on her dog. Occasionally I see robins on the roof of the shed, hopping around like they do. When my work runs deep into the night, I hear the robins start singing before dawn, and in the receding dark the sound is spellbinding."

waaseyaa'sin christine sy lives, loves, and laughs with her teen bear and queer cat on the tip of an island in the Coast Salish Straits. Published in various journals, this year her poems appear in *Gush: Menstrual Manifestos for Our Times* (eds. Rosanna Deerchild, Ariel Gordon, and Tanis Nielson) and "ndn country," a *CV2-Prairie Fire* collaboration guest edited by Katherena Vermette and Warren Cariou. She received the Lina Chartrand Award in 2014.

sy writes, "I wrote this poem in the season after my first visit to my deceased mother's lands and waters in the northwestern regions of Anishinaabewaki (Great Lakes watershed). Forty-four years' worth of yearning—and wisdom gleaned from the yearning—'my umbilical cord, map trail seasonal camp: a poetics of work' is at once a swan song of closure, new possibilities for maternal relationalities and a manifesto against both indigenous commodification of indigenous life in post-INM Canada and celebrious androcentric constructions of indigenous suffering. I wrote this poem on invitation to write for a collection on Northern Ontario poetics guest edited by Shannon Maguire and Lesley Belleau and I wrote this poem during the early months of living out of my territory. It is a thing to write home when away from it for the first time when you just visited it for the first time when living in a new home that are (is)lands and straits to the people of that place who didn't invite you to be there. This poem is a poetic cartographic anchor for a future self and for those who are making relational trails homeoutof home, too. My form intends to reflect a rhythm and breathe, a pause and period for what living indigenous looks like from one perspective. For bringing me here in so many ways, I say miigwech to my maternal family."

SOUVANKHAM THAMMAVONGSA was born in Nong Khai, Thailand, and raised and educated in Toronto, where she currently lives. Her writing has appeared in *Harper's*, *Granta*, and other places.

Of "Clown," Thammavongsa writes, "I wrote this poem because I hadn't seen a clown in a long time. When we are children, we don't notice the person behind the clown suit because they exist to make us things, they distract us with their tricks and training. Part of growing up is not being so distracted by someone's desire to make us happy, by the glitter, by the performance. And to ask if the person trying to make everyone else happy is happy themselves. The thing about a clown is if we ask those questions of them, then they would not be there in the first place."

ANNE MARIE TODKILL divides her time between Ottawa and Wollaston Township, Ontario. Her work has been anthologized in the *Best Canadian Poetry* series (2012 and 2015) and in *Best Canadian Stories* (2017). Her essays, fiction, and poems have appeared in various Canadian literary magazines, including *Arc Poetry Magazine, Canadian Notes & Queries, CV2*, and the *Malahat Review*. "November, Stormont County," was among the third-prize winners in *the New Quarterly*'s Nick Blatchford Occasional Verse Contest (2017).

Of "November, Stormont County," Todkill writes: "One thing about nature-watching: don't expect to see what you came for. Expect not to be ready when you do. There was nothing remarkable about a red-tailed hawk being where I saw it on the day described in my poem, but it seemed like a gift to me. And even if, to any analyst of eBird, the snow buntings were statistically likely, that's not foreknowledge—only hope. The snow geese weren't where I went looking for them, but on an unpropitious stretch of road I took as a short cut on my way home. Nevertheless, during the peak of the migration, the flat counties wedged between the Ottawa and the St. Lawrence are a pretty safe bet for those who, far from mountains or the sea, crave a dose of Big Nature. Just keep staring above the horizon. Geese will precipitate out of the distance—the ragged pulse of Canadas, the scintillation of Snows, half the time steering in directions that seem wrong. For me, it never gets old. But a recent wild goose chase had an odd result for my husband and me. Not far from the highway, a small flock of snow geese rested in a field. Two men walked among them; the geese didn't move. Something was up with this nature; we turned down the next concession, spied with our binoculars. A field of decoys. A little wiser, now we know: suited up in white coveralls, we could lie on our backs among an outfitter's fake birds, waiting to deal nature our own surprise. That's the other thing about nature-watching: humans are mixed up in it, too."

SARAH TOLMIE lives in Kitchener, Ontario. She is a speculative and historical fiction author and poet. Her poetry collection *Trio* was shortlisted for the Pat Lowther Award in 2016, and her newest collection is *The Art of Dying*, published by MQUP in 2018. Fiction publications include *The Stone Boatmen* (2014), *NoFood* (2014) and *Two Travelers* (2016), all with Aqueduct Press.

Of "On Seeing an Ad for Vaginal Rejuvenation in *Grand Magazine*,"

Tolmie writes, "This poem came to me, exactly as the title says, after seeing an ad for cosmetic surgery in my local home and style magazine. It said so much, so economically, about the magazine's readership (including myself). And it really is true that there is a genre of early French poems that feature *cons parlatz* (talking vaginas)."

CHRISTOPHER TUBBS, like his mother, is a member of the Mississaugas of the New Credit First Nation. He is moved by the hardships that his family has endured on the reserve and in the residential school system. Their experiences inspire nearly all of his work. Some of his works have previously appeared in the *Capilano Review*. He lives in New Westminster, BC.

Of "Customs Declaration to a White Empire," Tubbs writes, "I had been reading an anthology of Canadian short stories. One of them was Thomas King's 'Borders,' a story about a Blackfoot woman who, when attempting to cross the border between the United States and Canada, refuses to self-identify as 'Canadian' to the border guards. I had just returned from an extended stay in the United States myself; I began to reflect on all the mundane, bureaucratic ways that Western governments exert themselves on the lives of the conquered. One of the little details of the border crossing process that has always stuck with me is the little Canadian customs declaration form. I pulled up a copy of the form on my computer, meditated for a little bit, and answered the questions on the form. With a little tweaking, those answers became this poem."

DANIEL SCOTT TYSDAL lives in Toronto. He is the ReLit Award winning author of three books of poetry, the poetry textbook *The Writing Moment: A Practical Guide to Creating Poems* (Oxford University Press), and the TEDx talk, "Everything You Need to Write a Poem (and How It Can Save a Life)." He is an Associate Professor at the University of Toronto Scarborough.

Of "A MAD Fold-In Poem," Tysdal writes, "In late January 2017, I became mentally sick with a severity I had not experienced in years. It was an awful combo of mania, depression, and suicidal ideation. One sleepless night, I scribbled a line about my internal, self-tormenting voice being like fire, and this line became the start of a poem that figured this death-demanding voice as an artist and me as its medium. By Tuesday morning, I had not recovered, but I went to work and then to my reading at Bänoo Zan's Shab-e She'r (Poetry Night). Together, these experiences saved me. As I led my two creative writing workshops, my inner voice ranted and hated and raged against me, but I was buoyed by the students and their creativity, dedication, and generosity. At Shab-e She'r, I was lifted by my fellow readers and, after I broke down during my reading, embraced by the audience in hugs and honest conversations about suicide. I returned to my poem about my sickness and self-tormenting voice, then added a turn inspired by all of the amazing creators who sustain me and who I am stirred to sustain. The MAD fold-in, I thought, was the perfect form for exploring and preserving this experience because of its apt name, the way its fold brings the fringe to the centre, and the way it moves readers to take hold of the poem and create an embrace through the page."

KATHERENA VERMETTE is a Métis writer from Treaty One territory, the heart of the Métis nation, Winnipeg, Manitoba, Canada. Her first book, *North End Love Songs* (The Muses Company) won the Governor General's Literary Award for Poetry. Her novel, *The Break* (House of Anansi), was bestseller in Canada and won multiple awards, including the Amazon.ca First Novel Award. Her second book of poetry, *river woman*, will be published in Fall 2018 (House of Anansi).

Of "when Louis Riel went crazy" Vermette writes, "I don't know when, or if, LR ever went 'crazy.' There are many rumours and theories around his supposed breakdowns. There also seems to be dispute over when he took the name 'David,' as he didn't start signing it to his letters until May 1876, after his purported 'Washington epiphany.' Any historical inaccuracies in this poem, and there are many, are my own. My poet-brain, as I call it, seems to constantly muddle 'facts' in the search for 'truth.'"

SHERYDA WARRENER is originally from Grimsby, Ontario, and now lives in Vancouver. She is the author of two poetry collections: *Hard Feelings* (Snare, 2010) and *Floating is Everything* (Nightwood, 2015). Her work can be found online or in print in *Event, Grain,* the *Fiddlehead, Hazlitt,* the *Believer,* and others. In 2017, she was the recipient of the *Puritan*'s Thomas Morton Memorial Prize for poetry. Warrener teaches in the Creative Writing program at the University of British Columbia, and facilitates Artspeak Gallery's *Studio for Emerging Writers.*

Of "Unpredicatable Intervals" Warrener writes, "I was reading about this clock designed to tick for 10,000 years, with chimes scheduled to ring randomly every millenium, never repeating the same sequence of notes. How to reconcile these external off-rhythms with the internal and domestic patterns that create a structure to my days? That's what the poem attempts to interrogate with its own imbalances of sound and image. I like disturbing my own conventional notions of time, and playing with shifts in scale, which in this poem meant moving from the safety of my kitchen to the wild expanse of desert in only a couple of lines. All along, I'm noticing the time my body keeps, and how little control I have over its eventual decline."

IAN WILLIAMS lives in Vancouver. He is the author of *Personals*, shortlisted for the Griffin Poetry Prize and the Robert Kroetsch Poetry Book Award; *Not Anyone's Anything*, winner of the Danuta Gleed Literary Award for the best first collection of short fiction in Canada; and *You Know Who You Are*, a finalist for the ReLit Prize for poetry. His first novel, *Reproduction*, is forthcoming from Random House. Williams teaches poetry at the University of British Columbia. www.ianwilliams.ca

Williams writes, "'Cart' takes its title from the expression 'cart before the horse,' to address a relationship that has advanced too quickly: 'were skins By the sixth time / we met we.' What is happening here? Each sentence seems to begin in the middle and end in the middle. The standard syntax in English is subject-verb-object or, in other words, subject-predicate. In 'Cart,' I place the predicate before the subject, the cart before the horse, to imitate the relationship's disordered haste. A sentence such as, 'When removing my socks I held the handle of the oven for balance' becomes 'held the handle of the oven for balance When removing my socks I.' The subject 'I' comes last. It's not a perfect poem. The cart breaks down sometimes. Second point: There is a social argument being made by demoting subjects from their primary positions. The rest of the sentence, the parts usually placed last, gains prominence. Finalement, you'll notice the invention of a new punctuation mark in the poem's final stanza that combines a period, a colon, and an em-dash."

CATRIONA WRIGHT lives in Toronto. She is the author of *Table Manners* (Véhicule Press, 2017). Her poems have appeared in *Prism International*, *Prairie Fire*, *Fiddlehead*, *Lemon Hound*, *The Best Canadian Poetry 2015*, and elsewhere. She is the poetry editor for *the Puritan* and a co-founder of Desert Pets Press.

Wright writes, "I don't remember the exact origin of 'Origin Story.' I keep notes on my phone—stray observations, images, riffs on words and sounds, quotations from books or ads, movie and restaurant recommendations, deadlines, grocery lists. Here is a sample: 'July 6th! Provisional report. Polar sea on Monday. Every kernel of popcorn a controlled explosion. She exhausts herself laughing. Star anise and nutmeg and cottage cheese.' One day, feeling uninspired, I scrolled through this verbal junk heap in search of a spark. I found it in this equation: 'Origin Story = universal? = super literal = sex.' After reading this prompt from a former self, I wrote 'Origin Story' quickly, the lines tumbling out as couplets, an almost inevitable formal choice for a poem about copulation. Writing a near-complete draft in one go is unusual for me, and I think it explains the energy and urgency in the poem."

NOTABLE POEMS OF 2017 ⚘

Selected by the editors (in alphabetical order by author's name)

Afuwa and Dion Kaszas	"stitching back the land" *The Capilano Review* 3.31
Simina Banu	"our ancestors decided the symbol of silence would be a sword" *filling Station* 67
Gwen Benaway	"Reconciliation" *Arc Poetry Magazine* Fall 2017
Lisa Bird-Wilson	"City Slickers" *The Malahat Review* Winter 2016 77
listen chen	"You Can't See Your Face in Running Water" *The Capilano Review* 3.30
Margaret Christakos	"charger 10" *Lemon Hound* Oct 10, 2017
Jan Conn	"Partial Cloud" *Fiddlehead* 270
Jen Currin	"Dear Healing Walk" *filling Station* 66
Adebe DeRango-Adem	"déjà voodoo" *Minola Review* 2017
Darrell Epp	"On Our Way to Somewhere" *Event* 46
Paola Ferrante	"These Things She Wants" *Minola Review* 2017
Aaron Giovannone	"Nonnets 14, 15, 22, 23" *Arc Poetry Magazine* Summer 2017
Cornelia Hoogland	"Saint Marion in the Forest" *Hamilton Arts & Letters*
Marcela Huerta	"Tropico" *Lemon Hound* Sept 21, 2017
Sarah Kabamba	"how to forget a language" *The New Quarterly* 143
Ben Ladouceur	"The Burning Tree" *Poetry Magazine* ccxi
Fiona Tinwei Lam	"The Test" *The New Quarterly* Fall 2017
Richard P. LaRose	"Gravitas" *Prism* 55.2
Andrea Ledding	"child at Batoche, 2010" *Room* 40.2
Tanis MacDonald	"River Lot" *Arc Poetry Magazine* Fall 2017

Sadie McCarney	"Dick Van Dyke is a crackerjack wizard" *NewPoetry* September 5, 2017
Margaret McKeon	"broken and the bone marrow is laughing" *NewPoetry* September 19, 2017
rob mclennan	"from The Book of Smaller" *Touch the Donkey* 15
Cara-Lyn Morgan	"Hummingbird" *Hamilton Arts & Letters* 10.2
Erín Moure	"TR-Lating Wilson Bueno", *Vallum* 2.24
Samantha Marie Nock	"pākahamakew" *GUTS* May 29, 2017
Sina Queras	"Stings" *The Malahat Review* 198, Spring 2017
Ben Robinson	"The Sesquicentennial Luncheon" *Hamilton Arts and Letters* 10.2
Shaun Robinson	"Pilgrims" *The Malahat Review* Winter 2016
Janet Rogers	"Into Out of the Woods" *Canadian Literature* 230/231
Sarah Scout	"Paper dreams of my mother" *Numéro Cinq* Vol. VIII, No. 2
Adam Sol	"Makes Firm Our Steps" *Fiddlehead* 270
Karen Solie	"The Sharing Economy" *Granta* 141
Claire Marie Stancek	"PASSED UNDER WOODS, SHADE OF" *Cosmonauts Avenue* 2017
Steven Takatsu	"Night, Sleep, Death, and the Stars" *Prism* Fall 2017
Laurelyn Whitt	"Adagio in Churchill, 2016" *Grain* Fall 2017
Deanna Young	"Tiny" *Arc Poetry Magazine* Summer 2017
Jan Zwicky	"Armchair" *Arc Poetry Magazine* Winter 2017

MAGAZINES CONSULTED FOR THE 2018 EDITION ⁜

Augur Magazine. augurmag.com

The Antigonish Review. PO Box 5000, Antigonish, NS B2G 2W5. antigonishreview.com

Arc Poetry Magazine. PO Box 81060, Ottawa, ON K1P 1B1. arcpoetry.ca

Brick. PO Box 609, Stn. P, Toronto, ON M5S 2Y4. brickmag.com

Bywords. bywords.ca

Canadian Broadcasting Corporation, CBC Poetry Prize finalists. cbc.ca

Canadian Literature. University of British Columbia, 8-6303 N.W. Marine Dr., Vancouver, BC V6T 1Z1. canlit.ca

Canadian Notes & Queries. 1520 Wyandotte St. East, Windsor, ON N9A 3L2. notesandqueries.ca

Canthius. canthius.com

The Capilano Review. 102-281 Industrial Ave., Vancouver, BC V6A 2P2. thecapilanoreview.ca

Carousel. UC 274, University of Guelph, Guelph, ON N1G 2W1. carouselmagazine.ca

Carte Blanche. carte-blanche.org

C magazine. PO Box 5 Stn B, Toronto ON, M5T 2T2. Cmagazine.com

Contemporary Verse 2 (CV2). 502-100 Arthur St., Winnipeg, MB R3B 1H3. contemporaryverse2.ca

Cosmonauts Avenue. cosmonautsavenue.com

Dalhousie Review. Dalhousie University, Halifax, NS B3H 4R2. dalhousiereview.dal.ca

echolocation. echolocationmagazine.com

enRoute Magazine. Spafax Canada, 4200 Boul. Saint-Laurent, Ste. 707, Montréal, QC H2W 2R2. enroute.aircanada.com

Event. PO Box 2503, New Westminster, BC V3L 5B2. www.eventmagazine.ca

Exile Quarterly. Exile/Excelsior Publishing Inc., 170 Wellington Street West, PO Box 308, Mount Forest, ON N0G 2L0. theexilewriters.com

Existere. Vanier College 101E, York University, 4700 Keele St. Toronto, ON M3J 1P3. yorku.ca/existere

The Fiddlehead. Campus House, University of New Brunswick, 11 Garland Ct., PO Box 4400, Fredericton, NB E3B 5A3. thefiddlehead.ca

Fieldstone Magazine. fieldstonereview.usask.ca

filling Station. PO Box 22135, Bankers Hall, Calgary, AB T2P 4J5. fillingstation.ca

Forget Magazine. 810-1111, Melville St., Vancouver, BC V6E 3V6. forgetmagazine.com

Freefall Magazine. 460, 1720, 29th Street West, Calgary, AB T2T 6T7. freefallmagazine.ca

Geist. Suite 210, 111 W. Hastings St., Vancouver, BC V6B 1H4. geist.com

Grain. PO Box 3986, Regina, SK S4P 3R9. grainmagazine.ca

Granta. 12 Addison Avenue, London, UK W11 4QR. granta.com/issues/granta-141-canada

HA&L (Hamilton Arts & Letters Magazine). halmagazine.wordpress.com

Hazlitt. penguinrandomhouse.ca/hazlitt

The Humber Literary Review. humberliteraryreview.com

The Impressment Gang. theimpressmentgang.com

Juniper Poetry. juniperpoetry.com

The Leaf. PO Box 2259, Port Elgin, ON N0H 2C0. brucedalepress.ca

Lemon Hound. lemonhound.com

The Literary Review of Canada. 100 King Street West, Suite 2575, PO Box 35, Station 1st Canadian Place, Toronto, ON M5X 1A9. reviewcanada.ca

Maisonneuve. 1051 boul. Decarie, PO Box 53527, Saint Laurent, QC H4L 5J9 maisonneuve.org.

The Malahat Review. University of Victoria, PO Box 1700, Stn. CSC, Victoria, BC V8W 2Y2. malahatreview.ca

Maple Tree Literary Supplement. 1103-1701 Kilborn Ave., Ottawa, ON K1H 6M8. mtls.ca

Matrix. 1455 Blvd. de Maisonneuve, Montreal, QC H3G 1M8. matrixmagazine.org

Minola Review. minolareview.ca

New Poetry. newpoetry.ca

The New Quarterly. St. Jerome's University, 290 Westmount Rd. N, Waterloo, ON N2L 3G3. tnq.ca

Numéro Cinq. numerocinqmagazine.com

One Throne. onethrone.com

ottawater. ottawater.com

Our Times. 407-15 Gervais Dr., Toronto, ON M3C 1Y8. ourtimes.ca

(parenthetical). wordsonpagespress.com/parenthetical

Partisan. partisanmagazine.com

Poetry Is Dead. 5020 Frances St., Burnaby, BC V5B 1T3. poetryisdead.ca

Poetry. 61 West Superior St., Chicago, IL USA 60654. poetryfoundation.org/poetrymagazine

Prairie Fire. 423-100 Arthur St., Winnipeg, MB R3B 1H3. prairiefire.ca

PRISM International. Creative Writing Program, University of British Columbia, Buchanan Room E462, 1866 Main Mall, Vancouver, BC V6T 1Z1. prismmagazine.ca

Pulp Literature. pulpliterature.com

The Puritan. puritan-magazine.com

Queen's Quarterly. Queen's University, 144 Barrie St., Kingston, ON K7L 3N6. queensu.ca/quarterly

The Quilliad. thequilliad.wordpress.com

Ricepaper. PO Box 74174, Hillcrest RPO, Vancouver, BC V5V 5L8. ricepapermagazine.ca

Room. PO Box 46160, Stn. D, Vancouver, BC V6J 5G5. roommagazine.com

The Rotary Dial. therotarydial.ca

The Rusty Toque. therustytoque.com

17 Seconds. ottawater.com/seventeenseconds

The Steel Chisel. thesteelchisel.ca

subTerrain. PO Box 3008, MPO, Vancouver, BC V6B 3X5. subterrain.ca

Taddle Creek. PO Box 611, Stn. P, Toronto, ON M5S 2Y4. taddlecreekmag.com

This Magazine. 417-401 Richmond St. W, Toronto, ON M5V 3A8. this.org

Vallum. 5038 Sherbrooke W., PO Box 23077, CP Vendome, Montreal, QC H4A 1T0. vallummag.com

The Walrus. 411 Richmond St. E., Suite B15, Toronto, ON M5A 3S5 walrusmagazine.com

Windsor Review. Department of English, University of Windsor, 401 Sunset Ave., Windsor, ON N9B 3P4. windsorreview.wordpress.com

Untethered. alwaysuntethered.com

Zouch Magazine. zouchmagazine.com

Note: The Best Canadian Poetry series makes every effort to track down Canadian journals that publish poetry. The series relies on complimentary copies from the publications involved and is most grateful for cooperation. If you are the editor or publisher of a magazine not listed and wish to be considered for future years, please write to bestcanadianpoetry@gmail.com.

INDEX OF AUTHORS ✑

ACKNOWLEDGEMENTS ❧

"African Canadian in Union Blue" appeared in *enRoute* copyright © 2017 by Michael Fraser. Reprinted with permission of the author.

"After Samiya Bashir's Field Theories" appeared in *The Puritan* copyright © 2017 by Eli Tareq Lynch. Reprinted with permission of the author.

"The Amerindian in the Godzilla Suit" appeared in *Arc Poetry Magazine* copyright © 2017 by Daniel David Moses. Reprinted with permission of the author.

"Anonymous Woman Elegy" appeared in *carte blanche* copyright © 2017 by Tess Liem. Reprinted with permission of the author.

"As If Our Future Past Bore a Bad Algorithm" appeared in *CV2* copyright © 2017 by Liz Howard. Reprinted with permission of the author.

"Astronaut Family" appeared in *Canadian Literature* copyright © 2017 by Shazia Hafiz Ramji. Reprinted with permission of the author.

"Belittle" appeared in *Hamilton Arts & Letters* copyright © 2017 by Yusuf Saadi. Reprinted with permission of the author.

"From *THE BLUE CLERK*" by Dionne Brand. Copyright © 2018, Dionne Brand, used by permission of The Wylie Agency (UK) Limited. Selection from *THE BLUE CLERK* originally appeared in Granta Magazine. Revised poem selections appear in Dionne Brand's collection, *The Blue Clerk* (McClelland & Stewart, 2018).

"boneknockers" appeared in *The Antigonish Review* copyright © 2017 by Margaret McLeod. Reprinted with permission of the author.

"The Canada Goose" appeared in *The Malahat Review* copyright © 2017 by Mike Chaulk. Reprinted with permission of the author.

"Cart" appeared in *The Rusty Toque* copyright © 2017 by Ian Williams. Reprinted with permission of the author.

"CII" appeared in *Prism* copyright © 2017 by Sonnet L'Abbé. Reprinted with permission of the author.

"Clown" appeared in *The Rusty Toque* copyright © 2017 by Souvankham Thammavongsa. Reprinted with permission of the author.

"Come the Ungulate" appeared in *The Malahat Review* copyright © 2017 by Arleen Paré. Reprinted with permission of the author.

Biblioasis gratefully acknowledges the authors and publishers for permission to reprint the copyrighted works in this book. Every effort has been made to obtain permission for the use of copyrighted material. The publisher apologizes for any errors or omissions in the above list and would be grateful if notified of any corrections so that acknowledgement may be made in subsequent editions.

EDITOR BIOGRAPHIES ❧

HOA NGUYEN was born in the Mekong Delta, raised in the Washington, DC area, and lives in Toronto. From Wave Books, her poetry collections include *As Long As Trees Last*, *Red Juice: Poems 1998-2008*, and *Violet Energy Ingots*, nominated for a 2017 Griffin Poetry Prize. She teaches poetics at Ryerson University, for Miami University's low residency MFA program, for the Milton Avery School for Fine Arts at Bard College, and in a long-running, private workshop.

AMANDA JERNIGAN is the author of three collections of poetry—*Groundwork*, *All the Daylight Hours*, and *Years, Months, and Days*—and of the chapbook *The Temple*. Her poems have appeared in journals in Canada and abroad, including *Poetry*, *PN Review*, *the Walrus* and *the Nation*; they have also been set to music, most recently by American composer Zachary Wadsworth. She is an essayist and editor as well as a poet, and has written for the stage.

ANITA LAHEY is the author of *The Mystery Shopping Cart: Essays on Poetry and Culture* (Palimpsest Press, 2013) and of two Véhicule Press poetry collections: *Out to Dry in Cape Breton* (2006) and *Spinning Side Kick* (2011). The former was shortlisted for the Trillium Book Award for Poetry and the Ottawa Book Award. Anita is also a journalist and a former editor of *Arc Poetry Magazine*, and posts on her blog, "Henrietta & Me."